GREAT HOUSES
OF LONDON

James Stourton

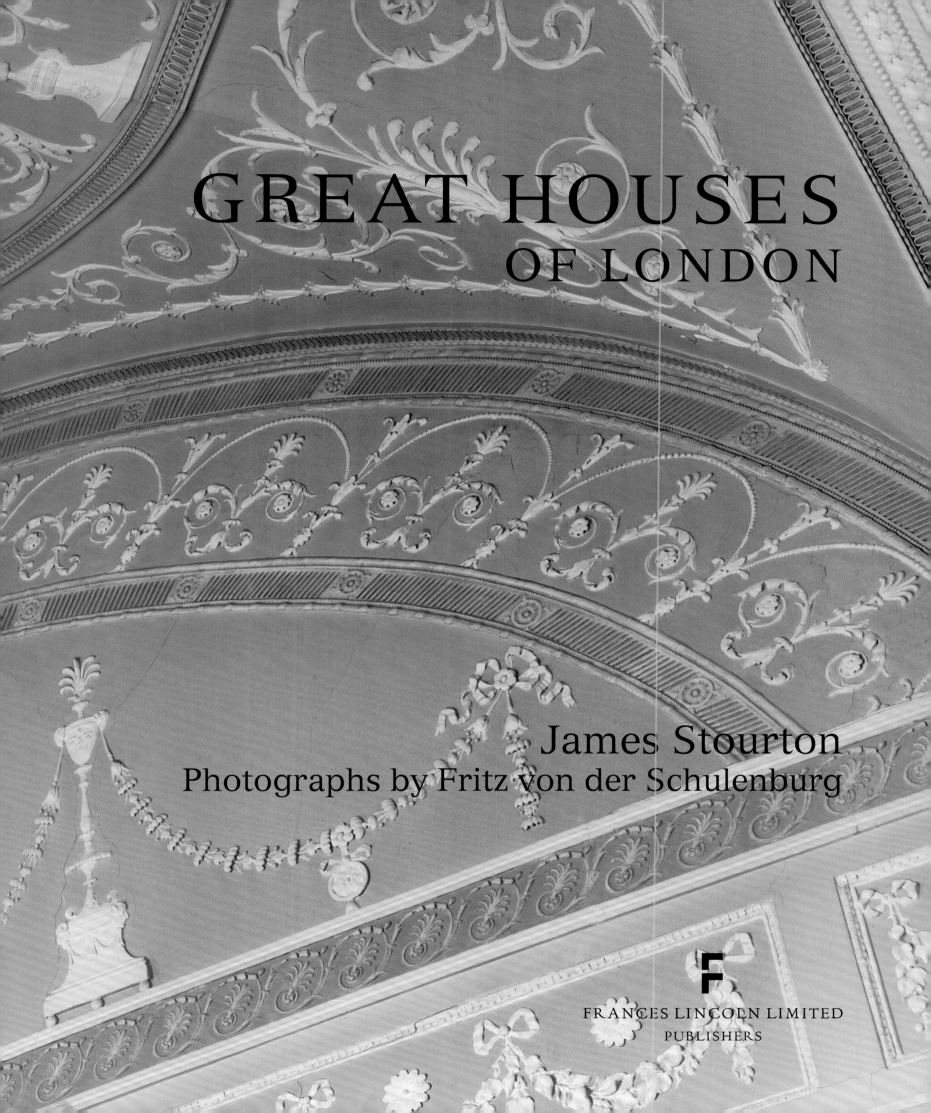

GREAT HOUSES
OF LONDON

James Stourton

Photographs by Fritz von der Schulenburg

F

Frances Lincoln Limited
PUBLISHERS

Frances Lincoln Limited
www.franceslincoln.com

Great Houses of London
Copyright © Frances Lincoln Ltd 2012
Text copyright © James Stourton 2012
Photographs copyright
© Fritz von der Schulenburg 2012
except for those listed on page 328
Index by Douglas Matthews

Designed by Becky Clarke

First Frances Lincoln edition: 2012

James Stourton has asserted his right
to be identified as author of this work
in accordance with the Copyright,
Designs and Patents Act 1988 (UK).

A catalogue record for this book is
available from the British Library.

ISBN 978-0-7112-3366-9

Set in Janson Text LT
Printed and bound in China

9 8 7 6 5 4 3 2

HALF-TITLE PAGE Richard
Rogers's 'piazza': the double-
height central living space in his
Chelsea house.
TITLE PAGE Robert Adam's
exquisite ceiling for
Lady Wynn's Dressing Room
at 20 St James's Square.
RIGHT William Kent's staircase
for 44 Berkeley Square.

CONTENTS

INTRODUCTION

This book is about three things: houses, architects and owners. The idea of writing it came to me one spring morning while walking through Green Park. At the eastern edge my eye roamed from Wimborne House down past Spencer House to Bridgewater House, Warwick House, Stornoway House, Lancaster House, and at the northern fringes to Coventry and Egremont; some more famous than others. How strange that there was no book that described them in their present circumstances. Their country cousins have consumed all the light and each year another book comes out which follows the same well-worn path. London houses have not been the subject of any such romantic adulation. While there is a group of famous London houses which have been well chronicled, there are far more that are unfamiliar. This is a reversal of the position in the eighteenth and nineteenth centuries, when London houses were generally better known than country houses.

The Great Houses of Paris, published in 1979, featured thirty-five *hôtels particuliers* and villas which demonstrated what everybody suspected: that the riches of surviving eighteenth- and nineteenth-century Parisian domestic architecture were extraordinary. How sad, I thought at the time, that, with so many houses demolished or blitzed, London could never compete with Paris on this front. Nearly every book on London houses seemed to reinforce this image of past glories in a lost landscape. Twentieth-century losses were indeed great, and have been well described in publications such as Oliver Bradbury's *The Lost Mansions of Mayfair* (2008). In the first rank: Norfolk, Londonderry, Grosvenor, Dorchester, Chesterfield, Aldford and Brook were grievous losses. The Blitz knocked about many houses, but surprisingly few were actually destroyed during the war. Holland House (really a country house) was a major loss and also Bridgewater House Gallery. What makes this book possible to write is the survival of that characteristic London dwelling, the terraced house. Frequently the lines are blurred – as at Wimborne House – between the free-standing palace and the terraced house. London more than any place on earth is the city of the terraced house.[1]

What are the rules of inclusion? Each house must have been built as a dwelling, and have been in metropolitan London at the time of building or during its period of greatest interest. This ruled out many agreeable country villas now absorbed into greater London. Cheyne Walk is debatable but the main interest in the story lies in the nineteenth century, by which time Chelsea had been subsumed into the metropolis. I have excepted royal palaces, although I include Marlborough House and Lancaster House, both with royal connections, because theirs is also an aristocratic story. There were further requirements. First, the houses needed to be photogenic, in order that their purpose should be fully understood; those that were converted to flats, gutted or empty would not feature. Second, each had to tell a good story. Certainly, things happened in London houses: half the Cabinet resigned after breakfast at Stratford House, the General Strike moved to its close at Wimborne House, Byron seduced Lady Caroline Lamb at Dover House, Archbishop Laud fought off the apprentices from Lambeth Palace, and George Moore dished out copies of Bunyan to taxi drivers at 15 Kensington Palace Gardens. It is only when we come to the present time that the story becomes harder to tell.

[1] Dublin and Edinburgh follow closely.

LEFT *Sculpture,* with a bust of Homer under her arm: a Coade stone statue by Flaxman for Buckingham Palace 1827–28, relocated to the garden of Lancaster House *c.*1913.

RIGHT The demolition of
Devonshire House in 1924
is often held to mark the
watershed: the point at
which the great aristocratic
families had to admit they
could no longer maintain
their London palaces.
OPPOSITE LEFT
The Jerusalem Chamber,
the Deanery, Westminster.
The timbers of the roof
bear the initials of Nicholas
Litlyngton (Abbot of
Westminster 1362–86) and
a crowned 'R' for Richard II.
OPPOSITE RIGHT
Matthew Brettingham's
Egremont House, once
home to Lord Palmerston
and later to the Naval and
Military Club (the In and
Out) is the only house in
this book currently in search
of a use.

This is often a matter of privacy and security. Where this has become particularly sensitive, as at Kensington Palace Gardens and the Regent's Park villas, I simply tell a generic story instead.

Tough choices had to be made. With 20 St James's Square and Home House the London story of Robert Adam is well told, and his admirable Chandos House, for instance, had to be excluded. Perhaps a greater problem was the number of houses in restoration, which made photography difficult. Debenham House, 15 Kensington Palace Gardens and Dudley House were all undergoing extensive work at the time of writing. The restoration of these and many other houses brings me to the curious realization that more of the great houses of London are back in private occupation today than at any time since World War II. This is particularly true of the Regent's Park villas, which is an international story. This is nothing new, and a close reading of this book reveals the foreign wealth from the 1850s that created or owned many of these houses. Today the likely occupants might be Arab royalty, Russian oligarchs or Indian billionaires, but the appetite for London houses at this level appears to be greater than at any period

since Edwardian times. It would be wrong to pretend that there are no casualties. Matthew Brettingham's Egremont House in Piccadilly is the very picture of mutability in its locked and forlorn state, a monument to the crashed dreams of its owner, who hoped to link it with Mentmore Towers in Buckinghamshire as a clubhouse for billionaires.

All of the houses in this book began as dwellings, but at least half of them changed their purpose at some point in their history. One of the most surprising discoveries is how short was the tenure of most families in these houses, depending on their need to keep up state in London and their financial position. The necessity of attending the season, Parliament or the court was usually the motivation to take the London lease. No. 7 Carlton House Terrace is a case in point, where the average residence was between five and ten years. The families who gave their names to palaces generally hung on as long as they could afford them. It is through the departure of these families that the story of London houses is often told. The destruction of Devonshire House in 1924 is usually taken as the point of crisis, although the 1930s were the most melancholy years involving demolitions.

Changes of use saved many houses. London houses have in fact been changing their uses ever since they were built. The most typical (if indeed it is a change of use) was to that of embassy: 106 Piccadilly, 6–9 Carlton House Terrace, Stratford House, Home House, 15 Kensington Palace Gardens and 46 Grosvenor Street were all at some point embassies, and several houses in the book hold that function today. Some changes of use, however brief, will come as a surprise. Who remembers that Marlborough House was the first home of both the Victoria & Albert Museum and the Royal College of Art; or indeed that Lancaster House housed the Museum of London? In the post-war period, Stratford House is a particularly busy example: few houses have changed their use so often. If the country house story is one of continuity, the London story is one of adaptation and change.

It is entirely fitting that the book opens with Lambeth Palace, on the river. Without the Thames there would be no London, and along its muddy banks arose the first great houses. Medieval buildings scarcely exist in London today. Those that survive often became private houses later, like the Charterhouse, or were uplifted, like Crosby Hall – which is now in Chelsea. It is the clergy houses, Lambeth Palace and the Deanery of Westminster – both beyond the reach of the Great Fire – that have the oldest claim to continuous private occupancy.

Beginning in the thirteenth century and reaching a climax during the sixteenth and seventeenth centuries, there arose the celebrated palaces along the north bank of the Thames, between the City of London and Whitehall, facing the Strand: the Savoy, Somerset House, Arundel House and Northumberland House, whose fame lives on in names, streets and the footprint of the present buildings on the site.

Nothing stimulated the westward growth of London so much as the Great Fire of 1666. Ashburnham House belongs to this period, though architecturally it is a country house. It is fitting that our next house is Marlborough House, because the 1st Duke's victories not only accelerated Britain's inexorable rise to world power but were also the catalyst for a burst of building in the city after the Treaty of Utrecht (1713).

Marlborough House is the earliest of the great London family houses to survive, but with 10 Downing Street (and

4 Cheyne Walk) we meet the vertical terraced houses created by speculative builders that were to be such an abiding feature of the London scene. The French chose to live horizontally in apartments and the British vertically in terraced houses. This is as much a cultural consideration as a practical one. Chief Justice Coke's ruling of 1628 'For a man's house is his castle, *et domus sua cuique est tutissimum refugium* [and each man's home is his safest refuge]' conditioned the idea and importance of having one's own roof. The longevity and pervasiveness of this form in London are remarkable and it accounts for almost half of the houses in this book. Cheyne Walk is characteristic of high-quality Queen Anne (or in this case early George I) houses, with red brickwork and beautiful carved wood doorways. By the next generation at William Kent's 44 Berkeley Square the bricks are grey (often yellowish) and the doorways made of stone. Kent, Robert Adam and John Soane

demonstrated how the terraced house could be taken to its artistic limits and in our own time Charles Jencks and Richard Rogers have rejuvenated the old form.

The great houses of London are largely the product of the great estates and the speculative builder. Since the 1630s, when the Earl of Bedford created Covent Garden, the square has been the central feature of London developments. The principal squares laid out in the eighteenth century were St James's, Hanover, Berkeley and Grosvenor. All except Hanover feature in this book. Grosvenor Square is but a pale shadow of its former self, and perhaps this is the moment to mention the Grosvenor Estate. In 1711 Sir Richard Grosvenor obtained an Act of Parliament to develop his Mayfair estate, but the building only began a decade later. Grosvenor Square, originally the work of Edward Shepherd, was the centrepiece of the estate. It contained many of

the finest mansions, which the Grosvenors proceeded to demolish in the 1850s to make way for Thomas Cundy's Italianate palazzi. No. 4 Grosvenor Square belongs to the Cundy phase; it survived the next round of rebuilding in the twentieth century because it was – and still happily is – the Italian Embassy.

Aristocratic families if they were shrewd, as in the case of the Bedfords and the Grosvenors, maintained ownership of the freeholds and granted leases of usually between fifty and a hundred years. The leasehold system did not always encourage solid building, let alone great architecture. Part of the continuous problem with the fabric of 10 Downing Street was that, in Winston Churchill's words, the house was 'shaky and lightly built'. As early as 1665 Lord St Albans was begging Charles II to grant him the freehold on St James's Square, 'for that men will not build Palaces upon any term but that of inheritance'.[2] The King agreed to his request, with the consequence that the fine houses were built in St James's Square such as those at No. 15 and No. 20 (albeit much later). It is nonetheless surprising how much fine architecture was constructed on leasehold plots.

The West End, defined today as the land between Park Lane, Regent Street, Oxford Street and the Mall, was to be the main area of aristocratic residence during the eighteenth and nineteenth centuries, and fourteen of our houses lie within these parameters. The lines were less clearly delineated in the eighteenth century, and 1 Greek Street represents a moment when Soho might have become aristocratic, before it succumbed to its role as the raffish buffer zone between the markets of Covent Garden and Mayfair. The creation of Regent's Street in the early nineteenth century was to firmly define the frontier. The brilliance of Mayfair was well expressed by Sydney Smith: 'I believe the parallelogram between Oxford-street, Piccadilly,

[2] Arthur Irwin Dasent, *The History of St. James's Square*, London 1895, p. 5.

LEFT Edward Shepherd's Crewe House on Curzon Street, now the Saudi Arabian Embassy.
ABOVE RIGHT The Palladian gallery at 12 North Audley Street, attributed to Sir Edward Lovett Pearce.
BELOW RIGHT Once the home of the Astors and now a club, Edward Shepherd's 4 St James's Square.

Regent-street, and Hyde Park encloses more intelligence and human ability, to say nothing of wealth and beauty, than the world has ever collected in such a space before.'[3]

We encounter the genius of William Kent at 44 Berkeley Square and Wimborne House but can here only salute in passing the admirable but less well known talents of the builder-architect Edward Shepherd, who was responsible for Grosvenor Square, Crewe House and 4 St James's Square. Both Kent and Shepherd are associated with the exquisite Palladian gallery that survives at 12 North Audley Street, but it is now attributed to Sir Edward Lovett Pearce. Matthew Brettingham provided the solid Palladian article at Coventry House and we can observe the transition from this style to the neoclassical at Spencer House. Lord Spencer's sacking of John Vardy in favour of James 'Athenian' Stuart becomes a familiar theme of London

building. When Stuart returned from his travels in Italy and Greece in 1755 he brought with him the rudiments of a new style of architecture. We can admire it internally on the first floor at Spencer House and externally in the Ionic facade of Lichfield House, at 15 St James's Square. Adam knew that he had to emulate this elegant neighbour when he designed 20 St James's Square.

The motivation for switching architects was usually one of style, replacing a previous fashion with a modern one. We witness this especially with Robert Adam, who replaced James Gandon at 20 St James's Square to provide his dazzlingly up-to-date interiors. After his return from Italy in 1758 Adam was a cuckoo in the architectural nest, taking over several older architects' country house projects. With the arrival of James Wyatt on the scene the tables were turned on Adam, who must have been particularly pleased therefore to have snatched Home House from his rival when the 'infernal

Countess' felt she wasn't receiving enough attention from the younger man.

The 1760s and 1770s emerge from these pages as a golden period when several of the most graceful houses in the book were built. This period also coincides with the emergence of the architectural profession as we recognize it today. A group of brilliant rival architects influenced the look of the West End: Robert Taylor, James Stuart, Robert Adam, and William Chambers, the architect of Melbourne House. Sir Robert Taylor, one of the most competent architects to have a hand in the development of Mayfair, built a number of excellent surviving houses such as Ely House and the neighbouring 3 Grafton Street. New and grander materials were employed. Spencer, Coventry and Stratford Houses were all built in Portland stone, which, except for the odd use of Bath stone, was to be the favoured material for the grandest houses until the fashion for stucco became established in the

1820s (with Carlton House Terrace, the Regent's Park villas, Seaford House, Kensington Palace Gardens).

From the 1790s it was less a case of one architect taking over another's project than the wholesale remodelling of existing houses. This is what Henry Holland provided for the Duke of York at Dover House and Benjamin Dean Wyatt for the Duke of Wellington at Apsley House. The falling out between Wyatt and the Duke over spiralling costs introduces another

OPPOSITE LEFT 'Athenian' Stuart's Lichfield House, 15 St James's Square: one of the earliest neoclassical facades in London.
OPPOSITE RIGHT Robert Taylor's graceful house for the Bishop of Ely, in Grafton Street.
ABOVE Melbourne House by William Chambers, long divided into apartments as Albany.

familiar theme of the story. B.D. Wyatt was notorious in this respect and his unbusinesslike ways caused the Sutherlands to replace him with Robert Smirke at Lancaster House. Smirke, like Robert Taylor and later Edward Blore, was one of the small band of architects whom the establishment committees loved, because they came in on budget.

The grandest houses in the book are the newly built great plutocratic palaces that emerge after the 1840s: Dudley House, Lancaster, Bridgewater and Seaford. Industrial wealth and land ownership fuelled this burst of architectural gigantism and it contained the seeds of its own destruction. Unlike the great country houses, these London houses had no economy of their own and required vast outside fortunes to support them. And it was outside fortunes that continued to drive the London plutocratic boom that lasted until World War I. Foreigners appear in the story from the 1850s: the South African Randlords, Indian maharajahs, German barons and American tycoons. Kensington Palace Gardens was from the beginning virtually a foreign domain. The Randlords preferred Park Lane and its environs. Joseph Robinson, for instance, went to live at Dudley House. The American Waldorf Astor wanted to be close to the City at Astor House on the Embankment, while Edgar Speyer preferred to be at the heart of Mayfair at 46 Grosvenor Street. The nineteenth-century Rothschilds are absent from this book. They made the west end of Piccadilly (Nos. 141 to 148) next to Apsley House their own – it became known as 'Rothschild Row' – but unfortunately most of their houses were demolished with the widening of Park Lane.

Music rooms were once a prominent feature of London houses. The most beautiful example is the Norfolk House Music Room, which is reassembled at the Victoria & Albert Museum. Dudley House, Seaford House and 46 Grosvenor Street still retain their former music rooms but that at Wimborne House, which doubled as a ballroom, was demolished when the house was modernized in the 1950s. The nineteenth century was the age of the picture gallery, which reflected the wealth of the great art-collecting families.[4] Apsley House, Lancaster House, Bridgewater House, Dudley House

[4] The pioneer was Thomas Hope's mansion (demolished 1851) in Duchess Street off Portland Place.

ABOVE A rare example of a Tudor revival London residence: Stanhope House on Park Lane.
BELOW The Norfolk House Music Room, designed by Giovanni Battista Borra, now at the Victoria & Albert Museum.

and Hertford House contain examples of spectacular galleries; they all survive, except that at Bridgewater House, which was destroyed in the Blitz.

The style of the Victorian and Edwardian rich was generally Frenchified Louis – Dudley, Lancaster, Apsley, Seaford; but could be Florentine – Bridgewater, 6 Carlton House Terrace and 46 Grosvenor Street (both Francophile and Florentine). Rarer was the taste for Tudor revival: Astor House at Embankment Gardens; and one could add Stanhope House, the extraordinary building on Park Lane next to the Dorchester Hotel. In the mid-nineteenth century the Grosvenor Estate was firmly Italianate, and under that flag rebuilt most of Grosvenor Square. However, the 1st Duke of Westminster, in the 1880s and 1890s, had a preference for the Queen Anne revival style and, probably under his influence, Lord Windsor chose the 'Wrenaissance' style for his late Victorian mansion on Mount Street.

In 1908 Beresford Chancellor wrote, in the last contemporary survey of London houses, *The Private Palaces of London*, that 'If we sought for one particular feature distinguishing London from the other capitals of Europe . . . it would probably be found in the number of its large houses, many of which are indeed the private palace that I have here called them.'[5] He compared them to the palaces of Venice, but noted that in London they still held their treasures and maintained their 'high estate'. It was the last moment that you could make such a claim, as the 1914–18 war hastened the end of the fortunes and the way of life that supported them. Taxation and death duties (imposed in 1894 and reinforced in 1910) precipitated a movement of the aristocracy to take themselves and their art collections to the country.

Great houses, however, mutate and if Mayfair was to become a commercial property kingdom in the twentieth century, the domestic story had already moved further west. We observe the development of Belgravia at Seaford House. In Belgravia, the Grosvenor Estate was able to impose a stylistic uniformity that, Grosvenor Square apart, was unobtainable in Mayfair. Architecturally it means that the whole is greater than the parts and there were surprisingly few candidates in Belgravia for inclusion in this book. The westward pull of London is evident at Kensington Palace Gardens, which was to be a story of the *nouveaux riches* rather than the aristocracy.

The most interesting new houses in Kensington, though, from the 1850s onwards are the Arts and Crafts houses and those belonging to artists and architects. This was a new development with earlier roots. We see the emergence of

[5] Beresford Chancellor, *The Private Palaces of London*, London 1908, p. ix.

the architect's own house at Sir John Soane's Museum from 1808 onwards.[6] The Museum of London, although it has never shown any interest in great houses, in 2001 put on the exhibition *Creative Quarters: The Art World in London 1700–2000*, on the subject of where and how artists lived.[7] One might have drawn the conclusion from the exhibition that it would be more profitable to buy an artist's house than their work. They were the pilot fish colonizing new districts of the city with their, invariably interesting, houses. I include two evocative examples: those belonging to Lord Leighton and Linley Sambourne.

But it is the architects who steal the show. The idea of architectural self-expression, creating a house that is both an advertisement and a monument, is marvellously illustrated by Soane's Museum, Burges's Tower House, Goldfinger's Willow Road, and, more recently, Richard Rogers's house in Chelsea and Charles Jencks's exuberant creation in Holland Park. Closely related are the 'art' houses which reflect their owner's aesthetic credentials. Both Debenham House and 64 Old Church Street demonstrate progressive impulses on the part of the patron.

The twentieth century as a whole, however, is a more fractured story. Important and attractive houses were built by Sir Edwin Lutyens and Norman Shaw, but most either have been converted to flats or were unsuitable for inclusion. The quality of the latter's Swan House is apparent from its exterior. Modernism raises its head in the Georgian and Victorian landscapes of Chelsea and Hampstead. 64 Old Church Street and 2 Willow Road are survivors when so many of their ilk have been altered by subsequent owners who did not share the totality of the architect's modernist vision. Perhaps the oddest survivor from the 1930s period is the surprisingly intact National Socialist interior by Albert

Speer on the Crown Estate at 6–9 Carlton House Terrace.

Post-war, the story is largely one of restoration and reaction to a disappearing London. Michael Inchbald rejected modernism at Milner Street and created his own style, using antiques alongside contemporary materials. The community restoration story at Spitalfields was to prevent further development by the City of London and preserve an area of Georgian property. Spitalfields and Malplaquet House bring the East End into the book and – that extraordinary spread of the 1980s – 'gentrification'. More effective planning controls made it harder for architects to build from scratch in London. The theme of new interiors behind old facades was an inevitable adaptation, used with great effect by Richard Rogers and Charles Jencks, who were able to realize their modernist and postmodernist visions respectively, while maintaining the integrity of the street.

Restoration was in the air during the 1980s at both ends of the property spectrum. At the grandest level, Lord Rothschild undertook his landmark conversion of Spencer House. It may be seen as a turning point when important London houses began to be regarded no longer as white elephants but as historic assets that could be both useful and enjoyed. For most of the twentieth century, the great London houses had been regarded as a liability. Eagle Star Insurance Company impeccably restored Wimborne House in the 1950s but only after they had failed to demolish it. One might contrast this attitude with that of Mike Lynch, who on acquiring the lease of 20 St James's Square in 2009 saw the benefit of being the only IT company in Britain to be housed in an Adam masterpiece. Attitudes change and users change. Great London houses have so far adapted surprisingly well to the conditions of the twenty-first century.

---

[6] Soane's master, Henry Holland, had a great mansion in Knightsbridge which was surely an inspiration.
[7] See also Kit Wedd, *Artists' London: Holbein to Hirst*, London 2001, published to coincide with the exhibition.

James Stourton
London 2012

USES IN 2012

MUSEUMS
Sir John Soane's Museum, Apsley, Leighton, Linley Sambourne, 2 Willow Road

CLUBS
44 Berkeley Square, 1 Greek Street, Home, Stratford, 4 St James's Square*

OFFICES
3 Grafton Street, Spencer, 20 St James's Square, Bridgewater, Astor, 46 Grosvenor Street, 6–9 Carlton House Terrace

EMBASSIES
Winfield, Kensington Palace Gardens (various), 4 Grosvenor Square, 54 Mount Street, Crewe*

*Illustrated in the introduction only

DWELLINGS
Regent's Park Villas (various), Kensington Palace Gardens (various), Dudley, 4 Cheyne Walk, Tower, Debenham, 64 Old Church Street, 10 Milner Street, Spitalfields (various), Rogers, Jencks, Malplaquet

EDUCATIONAL
Ashburnham, 106 Piccadilly

CHURCH, GOVERNMENT AND CIVIC
Lambeth Palace, Marlborough, 10 Downing Street, Mansion House, Dover, Lancaster, Seaford, Speaker's House

HOTEL
Wimborne

LAMBETH PALACE

Lambeth Palace is part of the enduring fabric of London. The Archbishops of Canterbury have owned the site since the twelfth century, and it has been their main residence since the thirteenth century. Royal dynasties have come and gone, the Civil War may have disrupted their tenure and World War II almost destroyed it, but the archbishops are still at Lambeth. The palace is also an office, a library and a landmark. To enter through the gatehouse known as Morton's Tower is to arrive at something akin to an Oxford college, ancient, learned, beautiful in parts, with an overall flavour of nineteenth-century collegiate architecture.

The twelfth-century monks of Canterbury, fearful of losing prestige, were horrified when Archbishops Baldwin and Walter began to create an alternative base at Lambeth. The Pope intervened to prevent them, but to no avail in the long run, since the political importance of their position demanded that the archbishops be close to Westminster.

Indeed, several, from Thomas Becket down to William Warham, served as chancellor.

The oldest surviving part of the palace is the Crypt or Undercroft built by Archbishop Langton (1206–28), which remains the most numinous part of the building. Because it is below ground level and was liable to flooding, the Crypt was used mainly for storage until it was reclaimed in the twentieth century. It has been a favourite of recent archbishops for communion services. The Chapel above is thirteenth century in origin but so rebuilt after World War II damage that it is a little cold, despite attempts to warm it up. John Betjeman, alluding to use rather than importance, fancifully called it 'the Church of England's Sistine Chapel'. It is characterized by plain vaulting, grey Purbeck shafts and very fine wooden stalls and screen installed by Archbishop Laud, that most unfortunate of prelates, in the 1630s. The woodwork was saved by being removed during the war.

LEFT The state and private apartments of the Archbishop of Canterbury in Edward Blore's new palace of 1829–31.

LEFT The gatehouse of *c*.1495, known as Morton's Tower.
BELOW The Chapel's Undercroft, the least altered part of the palace.
OPPOSITE The Guardroom housed the Archbishop's private militia after the Peasants' Revolt of 1381.

The red-brick gatehouse, perhaps the most familiar part of the palace, is known as Morton's Tower, after the archbishop who built it *circa* 1495. John Morton – famous for his 'fork' and taxes – had the young Thomas More in his household from the age of twelve. Morton's Tower contains some of the most atmospheric parts of the building, including the Audience Chamber that overlooks the entrance gate.

The fourteenth-century Guardroom, improbable in an ecclesiastical home, may have come about as a result of the

sacking of the palace during the Peasants' Revolt of 1381. It has served many functions: military (up to two hundred men in Laud's time – he had to repel five hundred London apprentices in 1640), dining room, then (after the Blore rebuilding in 1829–31) the setting for the First Lambeth Conference of Bishops in 1867, and home to evacuees of bombing in World War II. The Guardroom also introduces us to one of the main themes of the palace: episcopal portraiture. Rows of distinguished prelates in black and lawn white from the seventeenth and eighteenth centuries, painted by Hogarth, Reynolds, Romney, Dance and others, line the walls. The *Portrait of Archbishop Laud* is a copy of Van Dyck's original painting that hung at Lambeth. In his diary Laud recorded finding the portrait fallen on the floor and commented 'I hope this does not betoken some disaster.' He was arrested shortly after.

Archbishop Laud was executed in 1645 and his additions to the Chapel were vandalized during the English Civil War. With the abolition of the archbishopric and the occupation of the palace by Parliamentarian soldiers, this was the lowest point in its history until World War II. After the restoration of the monarchy and episcopate, Archbishop Juxon rebuilt the Great Hall between 1660 and 1663; it was described by Samuel Pepys as 'a new, old-fashioned hall'. By an unknown architect, the Great Hall of Lambeth is a glorious amalgam of a medieval hammer-beam roof with Restoration elements that include a soaring lantern. In the 1830s, as part of Blore's rebuilding of the palace, the important library was moved into the Great Hall and suitable neo-Jacobean bookcases were installed. It is one of the least known and most dramatic interiors in London.

Archbishop Howley, who was enthroned in 1828, has had the greatest impact on the look of Lambeth Palace in modern times. He is the archbishop seen in the celebrated painting *Queen Victoria Receiving the News of her Accession to the Throne*. Howley's architect, Edward Blore, was a competent if slightly dull architect who was known for always coming in on budget (which made him popular with committees). Blore reported that the existing building was 'miserably deficient' as the

residence 'of so distinguished a person like the Archbishop of Canterbury'. He built the main residential block, which contains the Archbishop's private and state apartments. Blore's friend Sir Walter Scott approved, describing it as 'in the best Gothic taste'. The architect used Bath limestone which, with the proximity to the railway, weathered badly; today the building has a rather bland refacing.

Internally Blore's rooms are fine and well proportioned. The entrance hall – with its screen which carries the upper-floor cloister – leads up the staircase to the corridor, painted dark red and hung with nineteenth- and early twentieth-century portraits including works by Lawrence, Sargent and De Lazlo. The pleasant but unremarkable state rooms include the State Drawing Room, with unexpected portraits of Cardinal Pole (as the last Catholic archbishop) and Sir Robert Walpole, and the State Dining Room, which displays the service commissioned by Howley for a dinner in honour of Queen Victoria. A note of cockney eccentricity is sounded in the so-called Polish Corridor, whose name derives from

LEFT The Great Hall of Lambeth, built 1660–63 by an unknown architect.
ABOVE The Audience Chamber over the main gate, in Morton's Tower.

panelling that required a polish. Here are displayed recent archbishops, including Robert Runcie who, on being told that the portrait did him justice, commented, 'It is not justice I need but sympathy!' The upper cloister continues the run of episcopal portraits round to Lollards' Tower.

Lambeth Palace suffered grievously in World War II. The Chapel and Lollards' Tower were almost destroyed and the roof of the Great Hall badly damaged. However, Archbishop Cosmo Lang recognized that he was not alone in his suffering and opened the palace to the devastated residents of Lambeth in their hour of need. After the war, Archbishop Fisher initiated a restoration programme of the palace which continued until the end of the twentieth century. Blore's ceiling in the State Drawing Room was put back only a decade ago. Lambeth Palace remains at the heart of the Anglican ministry and represents – with the exception of the Deanery of Westminster – probably the longest chain of continuous residence in the capital.

ABOVE Blore's staircase to the Archbishop's apartments.
ABOVE RIGHT Lambeth is a palace of corridors.
BELOW RIGHT Blore's State Drawing Room, which has views over the garden.
FAR RIGHT The Roman doorway of the Great Hall, dating from 1663.

ASHBURNHAM HOUSE

WESTMINSTER

At the heart of the beautiful muddle of old buildings that form a triangle between the Palace of Westminster and the Abbey lies Ashburnham House. Passing through Dean's Yard, under an ancient arch, we arrive at Little Dean's Yard, with Barry's House of Lords ahead and Hawksmoor's Abbey towers to the left. The weight of so much history is tempered by the fact that we are at the centre of a school and the yard echoes to the sound of teenagers laughing and playing football. Westminster School has been on the site since Tudor times. Ashburnham House sits in the middle of this historical aggregation, modest and dignified, the survivor of fire, schoolchildren and aerial bombardment.

The exterior of Ashburnham House, a mid-seventeenth-century U-shaped brick house with a rusticated front door, gives no hint of the glories within. The ground-floor rooms are marvellously sparse, with old panelling, stone floors and a few Elizabethan portraits. There has been a house here since the eleventh century but the earliest architectural remains are fifteenth century. In the following century, when the Abbey briefly became a cathedral, it became the deanery of the Abbey, until let in 1599 to Sir John Fortescue, Elizabeth I's Chancellor. The fireplace in the hall dates from this period. The house took its present form after 1662, when the lease was taken by Charles II's friend in exile William Ashburnham. The mystery has always been his architect. The problem lies in the fact that the tour de force of the house, the staircase, has the characteristics of Inigo Jones and John Webb and was attributed variously to one or other of them until fairly recently. The drawing room, on the other hand, is in the Restoration style and obviously from the 1660s. Today the house as a whole is attributed to a gentleman architect, William Samwell, working in the 1660s, who might easily have used earlier styles; the staircase suggests an amateur's inventiveness.[1]

[1] The attribution was originally made by John Harris.

LEFT The grand staircase from the 1660s, attributed to William Samwell.

BELOW The staircase with its extraordinary columnar gallery and lantern is the forerunner of many beautiful London staircases. OPPOSITE The sparse hall, presided over by Elizabeth I, who re-founded the school in 1560.

The staircase is one of the secret wonders of London, an imaginative response to an awkward space that is scarcely less thrilling than its successors at 44 Berkeley Square and Home House. The perspective, worthy of baroque stage scenery, rises to a Borromini-like oval columnar gallery and lantern. The scale and ambition of the lantern are extraordinary. The principal room in the house is the first-floor drawing room, light and lovely, with a fine Restoration ceiling. Today it is the school reading room, which is appropriate, for the rest of the floor is devoted to the school library, a series of fine rooms with eighteenth-century panelling.

The Ashburnhams lived in the house for three generations, until John, 1st Earl Ashburnham, sold the lease to the Crown in 1730, and it became a repository for the Cotton library of manuscripts, which had been presented to the nation in 1700. Shortly after their arrival in the house a fire broke out.

Dr Bentley, the King's librarian, was sleeping in the house at the time. His neighbour Dr Freind, the headmaster of the school, saw him rush out of the building in his wig and nightgown, clutching the *Codex Alexandrinus*. One hundred and fourteen manuscripts were destroyed and many others, such as the Beowulf manuscripts, still bear burn marks. The library was later to form one of the three founding collections of the British Museum.

In 1739 the Dean and Chapter purchased the house from the Crown for £500. It remained divided until 1881 as grace and favour houses for the sub-dean and a canon. Relations with the school were baleful throughout the nineteenth century and reached a nadir with the death of Sub-Dean Lord John Thynne, in 1881. After an acrimonious public debate, Westminster School succeeded in taking possession of Ashburnham House a year later.

The original school began as a training college for clerks to the Benedictine Abbey. It survived the dissolution of the monasteries and was re-founded by Elizabeth I along modern lines with forty scholars and fee-paying 'town boys'. The Queen's 1560 charter instructs that 'the youth which is growing to manhood, as tender shoots in the wood of our state, shall be liberally instructed in good books to the greater honour of our state.'[2] In this the school has been entirely successful, consistently producing great men, and latterly great women.

Ashburnham House made the adaptation to a school with ease. It had, however, had one more role to play. During World War II it became the Churchill Club, where American forces could borrow books and listen to music or lectures. T.S. Eliot, Kenneth Clark and many others performed there and a bomb fell nearby during one of Edith Sitwell's recitals. With its proximity to Parliament it was almost inevitable that the school would one day be hit, and on 10 May 1941 a raid destroyed several buildings – 'Whatever will the Bursar say?' remarked one college servant – but, miraculously, Ashburnham House was only grazed.

Today, sandwiched between the icons of Church and State, Ashburnham House remains at the heart of the school.

[2] John Field, *The King's Nurseries: The Story of Westminster School*, London 2007, p. 21.

RIGHT Looking from the anteroom into the first-floor drawing room, now the school reading room.
FAR RIGHT Most of the first floor is today devoted to the school library.

MARLBOROUGH HOUSE

PALL MALL

First a house, then a palace, now a headquarters, Marlborough House occupies a key position on the Mall, yet remains an enigma to most Londoners. 'The strongest and best house ever built' was Sarah, Duchess of Marlborough's verdict on her London home. The Duke had no great opinion of Marlborough House and preferred Blenheim. Love and ambivalence have been the story of Marlborough House ever since. Repeatedly altered and re-altered, the unfortunate house has never been sure to which century it belongs, and nor have its later inhabitants. Despite that, it has some of the finest and least known interiors in London. The spirit of the house belongs to two strong women, Duchess Sarah and Queen Mary. Today Marlborough House is beautifully maintained as the headquarters of the Commonwealth.

Sarah, Duchess of Marlborough, secured the lease of the site from Queen Anne in 1708 and instructed Sir Christopher Wren to build a house 'plain and cheap'. It was completed in 1711, a pleasant building – old-fashioned for its date – of only two storeys, in red brick with stone edging and no fashionable pediments or columns. The Duke acquired the bricks cheaply in Holland and his empty troop ships carried them home as ballast. The footprint of the house is unchanged, but to imagine Wren's house you must remove the second and third floors in your mind's eye. Sarah dismissed the architect, 'the poor old man', as she called him, believing that the contractors were taking advantage of him, and she took control herself. The only thing even she failed to achieve was a grand front entrance from Pall Mall. Wren's arch and screen still exist, but Sir Robert Walpole, Sarah's political foe, bought the adjoining plots in Pall Mall to deny her an entrance. Today the arch is a grotto, and the approach remains on an awkward diagonal.

Sarah lived on in the house for twenty-two years after her husband's death, an object of curiosity and awe who

RIGHT Wren's Blenheim Saloon, as decorated for the future Edward VII.

condescended to get along with 'my neighbour George'.[1] Internally, little survives from the Wren period except the Blenheim Saloon, its two pendant staircases and the old Dining Room, now aptly named the Wren Room. The Saloon is the showpiece of the house and stands at its heart. Although tarted up by the future Edward VII, the double-height cube

[1] George II at St James's Palace.

with its murals by Louis Laguerre is essentially eighteenth century. The most surprising element is the ceiling painting displaying the benefits of peace by Orazio Gentileschi (who may have been helped by his daughter Artemisia), originally painted for the Queen's House at Greenwich. It was installed at Marlborough House – probably as a gift of Queen Anne – to celebrate the Treaty of Utrecht (1713).

Flanking the Saloon are painted staircases by Laguerre, one representing the Battle of Malplaquet and the other the Battle of Ramillies. Unfortunately, they were the subject of an insensitive twentieth-century restoration. The two main pictures have been well restored, but some of the smaller ones are parodies of the originals; the culprit is said to be the famous forger Tom Keating, who was involved in the work.

After the death of Sarah, the house had a chequered history. The 4th Duke of Marlborough brought in Sir William Chambers, who added the third storey and some fine ceilings and chimneypieces. On the death of the 4th Duke in 1817 the Prince Regent took back the remaining lease for his daughter Charlotte and her husband, Leopold Saxe-Coburg-Saalfeld. When Charlotte died Leopold lived on at

LEFT Laguerre's murals of Marlborough's victories married to Gentileschi's ceiling from the Queen's House at Greenwich.

ABOVE Laguerre's painting of the Battle of Ramillies.

Marlborough House, and he accepted the throne of Belgium in the Saloon. Queen Adelaide then arrived, thus starting the tradition of dowager queens occupying Marlborough House, but with her death in 1849 we feel the hand of Prince Albert at work. The house was used to display two collections of paintings, the Vernon and Turner bequests (to be the germ of the Tate Gallery), and it became the first home of both the Victoria & Albert Museum and the Royal College of Art.

These were transitory uses and it was not until the marriage of Edward, Prince of Wales, to Princess Alexandra of Denmark that the house came into its own again. Extensive alterations were done from 1861 onwards by Sir James Pennethorne, who added another storey, and the monumental porte cochère. He also knocked together ground-floor rooms to create grand entertaining areas for the Prince and Princess. The house was elaborately done up for the royal couple and a household of over a hundred staff effectively maintained an alternative court at Marlborough House. A Scottish gillie in Highland dress would greet visitors. The Prince wanted it to be 'the best kept house in London' – even though many thought it had the worst morals. The Marlborough House set, which consisted of a somewhat risqué group, including racing swells, bankers and other plutocrats, became a byword for fast living, to the point that a group of pious ladies canvassed the Archbishop of Canterbury about it. The term 'Marlborough House set' became current in the 1880s to denote the raffish world the Prince inhabited, in stark contrast to his widowed mother's staid court up the road.

The Prince's den was on the first floor, a panelled study lined with shelves bearing imitation book spines with such humorous titles as *The Wheel of Life* by Stopit and *Spare the Tree* by Y. Hewitt. He cluttered the house to such an extent that when he became King and moved to Buckingham Palace, his daughter-in law, Princess (later Queen) Mary called it 'that filthy, dirty house'. She had a gift for doing up rooms and made Marlborough House a comfortable family home where her children (two of whom were to become kings) were brought up. Her redecoration upset the King, who felt that what was good enough for him should be good enough for her. When it was her turn to move up the road as Queen she wrote to her eldest son that Buckingham Palace 'is not so *gemütlich* as Marlborough House'. Queen Alexandra returned there, but when she died the Prince of Wales, the future Edward VIII, refused to move in. He preferred his bachelor pad at St James's Palace.

With the death of George V Queen Mary returned to the house and it was in her upstairs sitting room that the

new King informed her of his intention to abdicate. With the coming of war Queen Mary settled for the duration at Badminton. Marlborough House was damaged during the Blitz in 1940: windows were blown in, doors blown off their hinges, and some ceilings collapsed; but by and large it remained remarkably intact. When, post-war, Queen Mary returned, she, like Duchess Sarah before her, seemed to be a relic from another age, imperiously grand in her famous pearls and long dresses. She was the last royal resident, and she died in the house in 1953. Six years later the Queen put Marlborough House at the disposal of the Commonwealth. Today the Secretary-General is based there and, among many other things, organizes the great gatherings of Commonwealth heads of state every two years under the invitation of the Queen. Marlborough House has retained its air of majesty and seclusion.

ABOVE The arch of Sir James Pennethorne's forecourt.
RIGHT Pennethorne's magnificent State Dining Room.

10 DOWNING STREET

WHITEHALL

Is there a terraced house in the world more famous? Passing through the reinforced metal black door, the visitor enters a labyrinth of corridors and awkward progressions. The scale of the house becomes apparent, and its lack of coherent design. The false modesty of the entrance blossoms upstairs into a pleasant country house. No. 10 has been cobbled together and rebuilt more often than any other house in London. It would have been far cheaper to have pulled the house down and started again but that was never going to be an option, for 10 Downing Street above all stands for an idea. Steeped in history – more chequered than I imagined – the understated fabric of the house represents the way the British see themselves, and its survival through mobs, developers and wars has given it a totemic quality in national life.

The present No. 10 consists of two houses. At the back is a mansion overlooking St James's Park which was built in about 1677. In front of this, facing the street, is the house built by George Downing as part of the Downing Street terrace. It was the demolition of the Cockpit Theatre that created the space on which Downing secured the leases in 1682 to build the houses that Winston Churchill was later to characterize as 'shaky and lightly built by the profiteering contractor whose name they bear'.[1]

The connection between government and No. 10 was not made until 1735, when Sir Robert Walpole moved in as First Lord of the Treasury. George II had offered Walpole both No. 10 and the house at the back as a gift. In a rare moment of self-restraint, the minister accepted it not for himself but on behalf of the holders of the office. It was almost certainly Walpole who brought in William Kent to combine the two houses. Thus began the first of at least nine major overhauls of the house, all of which took much longer and cost far more than projected. Kent's work is largely obscured but it is to his

[1] Christopher Jones, *10 Downing Street*, London 1985, p. 32.

LEFT The famous door with the plaque: First Lord of the Treasury.

period and style that subsequent prime ministers have usually returned in their attempts to recreate an 'authentic' residence.

Walpole resigned in 1742 and it was twenty-one years before a first lord, or prime minister, again occupied the house. The street was a rackety backwater; Boswell had lodgings there and Tobias Smollett tried to establish a surgeon's practice in it. The most colourful eighteenth-century resident of No. 10 was Sir Francis Dashwood, Chancellor of the Exchequer, famous for his Hell Fire Club and pranks, 'to whom a sum of five figures was an impenetrable secret'.[2] The man who really established the house as the

[2] Ibid., p. 55.

residence of the Prime Minister was William Pitt. His was to be the longest occupancy (1783–1801, 1804–1806). He called it 'my vast awkward house', but also 'the best summer townhouse possible'. Although the so-called Great Repair took place over eight years during the 1770s, the builders were still needed in Pitt's time. Newspapers fulminated at the cost but, as usual, prime ministers indulged the house.

It was Frederick Robinson, in occupation as Chancellor of the Exchequer from 1823 to 1828, who made the most notable change to the house, by bringing in Sir John Soane to create two dining rooms in stained oak panelling, one for intimate family dining and one for state occasions.

OPPOSITE A country house in town, with its own rose garden.
LEFT Photographs of prime ministers ascend the staircase.

ABOVE The Pilllared Room is used for the Prime Minister's
receptions.

ABOVE RIGHT The Terracotta Room, with the ceiling and overmantel
installed by Quinlan Terry for Mrs Thatcher.
BELOW RIGHT The White Room opens the entertaining parade on
the first floor.

Lord Grey steered the Reform Bill of 1832 from No. 10 but was forced to move out for some years while yet more repairs were made. After Grey's resignation in 1834, eight prime ministers ignored the house (invariably they already owned better houses), but gradually during the nineteenth century the government bought up all the surrounding freeholds and completed a massive building programme of Foreign Office and Treasury buildings that had 10 Downing Street at its heart.

Disraeli moved into No. 10 for his second term of office and in 1877 installed a bath with hot and cold water. Rosebery (like Wellington before him) used the house chiefly to avoid building works in his own home. Salisbury – who held Cabinet meetings at the Foreign Office – lent the house to his nephew, Arthur Balfour, a bachelor who, like Pitt, adored the place. Balfour used the Cabinet Room as his study and hung Burne-Jones paintings in the State Dining Room. Balfour became Prime Minister in 1902 and from then on every holder of the office has lived and worked at No. 10. Central heating came in 1937, 'dreadful stuff' exclaimed the departing Mrs Baldwin, but the greatest challenge to the fabric came three years later with the Blitz. Bombs fell all around the heavily reinforced house. The Churchill family was the last to live in the state rooms, albeit spasmodically between raids and damage, and visitors to No. 10 invariably feel the spirit of Winston's indomitable personality.

Clement Attlee created the upstairs family flat after the war, but by the 1950s it was clear that the house was near collapse. A committee under Lord Crawford recommended a rebuild retaining the external design and internal historical features. A young classical architect, Raymond Erith, undertook the job in a remarkably self-effacing manner. His only exuberance was to put two giant Corinthian columns in the courtyard, like the remains of a protruding Roman temple.

Today the house exudes a quiet sense of power. The entertaining parade of state rooms is laid out on the first floor. Mrs Thatcher felt that these rooms were too plain and masculine and with the confidence of the afterglow of the Falklands War, she brought in Quinlan Terry, an Erith pupil, to provide heavily gilded ornamental ceilings and overmantels in a Kentian manner. The White Room, which comes first and is the primary room for meeting and greeting distinguished visitors, boasts two fine Turner paintings on loan from the Tate. The Terracotta Room follows, a warm room with Turkey rugs and mahogany furniture. The portraits in the room – apart from those of Wellington and Nelson – are a surprising medley, including a Raeburn of the physician James Hamilton, and John Constable's portrait of his niece. The Pillared Room is the main reception room: its yellow walls set off portraits of Elizabeth I, the Old Pretender and Lady Byron.

Without question the greatest surprise of Downing Street is the two Soane dining rooms. The State Dining Room with its panelling and starfish ceiling is an architectural marvel on a palatial scale, and it is pleasing to see that otherwise dismal monarch George II presiding. After this triumphant note the Cabinet Room created in 1796 is rather cramped. Even here there are surprises. Walpole presides, naturally enough, over a Kent fireplace but at one end are the remains of the library that the room once held. Two bookcases hold an array of books by native authors – Gibbon, Byron, Disraeli, Frazer's *Golden Bough*, Doughty's *Arabia Deserta* – and one visitor, Homer's *Iliad*.

William Pitt's 'vast awkward house' is lovable and eccentric, welcoming and absorbing of all premierships, but remaining itself.

ABOVE RIGHT Sir Robert Walpole still presides over the Cabinet Room.
BELOW RIGHT Raymond Erith's Roman temple.
FAR RIGHT Soane's State Dining Room, with its remarkable starfish ceiling.

WIMBORNE HOUSE

ARLINGTON STREET

Wimborne House has changed its name more often than any other great house in London, being called, at different times by its different owners: Beaufort House, Hamilton House, Eardley House and Wimborne House; it is known today as William Kent House, but we refer to it by the name it held longer than any other. There are many grander houses than Wimborne House, but few that are more representative of the changing ownerships and styles of London houses. The house has been internally remodelled six times, which gives it a complex architectural history. The home of two prime ministers and several dukes, Wimborne House also attracted the attention of writers, notably Osbert Sitwell and Evelyn Waugh. Today, as part of the Ritz, it is the grandest hotel extension in the world.

When Henry Pelham bought 22 Arlington Street in 1740, he demolished the existing seventeenth-century house and engaged William Kent. The architect set the new house back from the street behind gates, with an entrance to one side, which suited the unusually long site between Arlington Street and Green Park. The house ended up being halfway between a grand terraced house and a *hôtel particulier* with a forecourt.

Arlington Street was always a street of politicians. Horace Walpole – whose father, Sir Robert Walpole, lived in the street – called it 'absolutely the ministerial street'. When Pelham succeeded Walpole as Prime Minister in 1743 he decided to discharge his duties from his new house rather than from Downing Street. His premiership provided stable if unglamorous mid-century government and he had to deal with the twin difficulties of the Jacobite '45 rising and being George II's unwanted chief minister.

Entrance to the house was (until recently) through an arcaded gallery. The staircase is a noble space that has always had the misfortune to be compared to Bel Finch's staircase at 44 Berkeley Square, which Kent designed at much the

BELOW Kent's staircase with its sinuous balustrade.
OPPOSITE ABOVE Kentian magnificence in the Octagonal Room.
OPPOSITE BELOW The 1920s Oval Room in the Louis XVI style.

same time (see page 54). The original Great Room (now the Burlington Room) is on the first floor and overlooks the courtyard rather than the park. It has a fine Kent white and gold honeycomb ceiling. There are two other former reception rooms with Kent ceilings on this floor; they both overlook the park.

When Pelham's next-door neighbour, Lady Codrington, moved out in 1743 he was able to double his available space. Pelham's purchase of her house gave Kent the chance to do something spectacular. He brought the main parade of reception rooms down to the ground floor and created a new Great Room (later the Drawing Room and now the William Kent Room) that rises through the floor above. It was unfinished at Kent's death in 1748 and completed by his assistant, Stephen Wright. It remains the central feature of the house and is the richest room imaginable, with an elaborate and colourful ceiling not dissimilar to those at the Doge's Palace in Venice and the Villa Madama in Rome.

Pelham died in 1754, shortly after the completion of the house, and his heirs let the house to Earl Gower, who found it a convenient perching place while he was building his own palace on Whitehall. He was followed by the 3rd Duke of Grafton, who lived here during his premiership and behaved according to Horace Walpole as if 'the world should be postponed to a whore and a horse race'. Lord Lincoln, Pelham's grandson, briefly lived in the house, followed by the 4th Duke of Rutland. Then (1787–98) there came a fascinating change: Sir Sampson Gideon of Portuguese Jewish extraction.

Gideon's father, also called Sampson, was the economic advisor to Walpole and Pelham; he was known as 'the great oracle'. He kept his Jewish faith but brought up his children as Christians. The eldest of them, Sampson (later Lord Eardley), was given a baronetcy at the age of thirteen by George II as a mark of esteem for the father who, as a Jew, was ineligible for such an honour. Gideon hung his father's distinguished picture collection at Arlington Street and commissioned George Dance the Younger to create the Dining Room (now the Music Room). After a fire in 1978 the room was rebuilt in a pleasant Wyattesque style, with a shallow-arched ceiling resting on long pilasters.

The strangest alterations to the house were made by Henry, 7th Duke of Beaufort (in occupation 1838–53), who acquired the freehold and brought in the architect Owen Jones, the author of *A Grammar of Ornament*, and the Italian fresco painter Eduardo Latilla, to transform Arlington Street into a parody of Pompeii and Herculaneum – except for the Great

Room, to which he added bizarre medieval elements from the time of Henry IV. Even the artist thought a 'description might alarm'. Nothing remains of these curious decorations. Beaufort's successor, the 11th Duke of Hamilton, acquired the house in 1854 for £60,000 and used the Scots architect William Burn to build a conservatory and remodel the entrance.

The longest residence was by three generations of the Guest family, who were ironmasters in Wales. By the middle of the nineteenth century industry had supplanted agriculture as the main support for great London houses, and the Guests were typical of the new families who rose to prominence (although they also owned 80,000 acres of land in several counties). Ivor Guest acquired 22 Arlington Street in 1870 and engaged decorators George Trollope and Sons to modernize the house. They removed most of Owen Jones's decorative work and during the 1880s added the vast Ballroom in the heavily ornate Italianate style of the Devonshire House Saloon. Guest was created 1st Baron Wimborne in 1880 and changed the name of the house.

Trollope and Sons embellished the Great Room with inlaid doors, panelling, and a grotesque chimneypiece

ABOVE The lost Owen Jones decoration.
RIGHT The William Kent Room, twice restored in the post-war era.

Viscountess Wimborne was particularly interested in music and instigated a series of subscription concerts in 1932 that Lavery captured in his painting *Chamber Music at Wimborne House*. Lady Wimborne counted William Walton (twenty years her junior) among her lovers. Lord Wimborne was a *grand seigneur* and Osbert Sitwell thought his beautiful wife 'hid from the crowd the clever woman who inhabited this exquisite shell'.[2] Sir Osbert left a memorable description of one of the last great political houses. Winston Churchill was a regular visitor and – if Sitwell is to be believed – the talks that led to the settlement of the General Strike in 1926 were begun at Wimborne House.

During World War II the Red Cross occupied Wimborne House and in 1947 the family sold it to the Eagle Star Insurance Company for £250,000. Two years earlier, Evelyn Waugh had published his lament to the country house world, *Brideshead Revisited*, in which he also gave an elegiac description of Marchmain House, 'Marchers' as the fictitious Flyte family affectionately referred to their London home, which matches well with Wimborne House: 'forecourt, the railings . . . bays of windows opening into Green Park etc. . . .'. In Waugh's novel, Marchmain House is pulled down in order to make way for a block of flats. This happened to four adjacent houses in Arlington Street but Wimborne House survived. Eagle Star accepted that it was impossible to develop the site as they had hoped and restored the house instead. They built modern offices in the forecourt. The house was returned to its mid-eighteenth-century form with consequent loss of the Ballroom.

The present chapter of Wimborne House's history began in 2005, when the Ritz Hotel, the most architecturally distinguished hotel in London, acquired their venerable neighbour. They are a perfect match and the rooms, furnished and burnished, are used once more for entertainment. The purchase by the hotel was the realization of a century-old dream. Soon after the Ritz opened in 1898, an enquiry was made to Lord Wimborne as to whether he would sell the house in order to expand the hotel. The famous response was: 'I am thinking of enlarging my garden. How much will you take for the Ritz?'

and mirror. Beresford Chancellor, the historian of London houses, loved it: 'I do not know in London any apartment quite analogous to the Drawing Room [Great Room] at Wimborne House; others are larger and loftier: others are filled with gems of pictorial art which are here, perhaps wisely, absent; but no room, not even those more magnificent ones at Stafford or Dorchester House, reproduces quite in the same way the decorative glories of the Italian renaissance.'[1] Today the Wimborne additions are stripped away, the walls are covered in crimson damask (following the 1754 inventory) and the room is much as Kent designed it, if largely reconstructed.

Guest's son, 2nd Baron and 1st Viscount Wimborne, continued the modernization, giving various rooms the Louis XVI treatment. Some of these survive, as well as the chaste Oval Room by Thornton Smith and Co. from the 1920s which links the William Kent Room with the Music Room.

[1] Beresford Chancellor, *Private Palaces of London: Past and Present*, London 1908, p. 370.

[2] Osbert Sitwell, *Laughter in the Next Room*, London 1949, p. 213.

LEFT *Chamber Music at Wimborne House,* by Sir John Lavery, 1932.
ABOVE The lost 1880s Ballroom in the Louis XIV style.

44 BERKELEY SQUARE

MAYFAIR

Berkeley Square has a special place in the hearts of Londoners. Grosvenor Square has its millionaires, Belgrave Square its embassies, but Berkeley Square has its plane trees and its nightingale. It also holds, at No. 44, one of the architectural wonders of London. This house is an extraordinary example of what could be achieved by a great architect, working within a small space and for a client with limited means who had no need to accommodate a family. The architect was William Kent and the client Lady Isabella Finch. No. 44 is a miniature palace, a terraced house taken to its extremity of grandeur.

Berkeley Square was begun in the 1730s in what was called Berkeley Row on the east side of the square. The ownership of the square was with the Berkeley family, except for the northern end, which was part of the Grosvenor Estate. The south side was taken up with the gardens of Lansdowne House. It is the west side that contains all the interest and, in particular, the short parade of houses from No. 44 to No. 47 is outstanding.

Lady Isabella Finch was one of the seventeen children of the 2nd Earl of Nottingham and 7th Earl of Winchelsea. The members of this family were famous for their dark complexions; they were known as the 'dark funereal Finches'. Lady Isabella, always called 'Bel', never married. Instead she acted as lady-in-waiting to the two unmarried daughters of George II; they could be tactless and Lady Bel would smooth the ruffled feathers. She attracted intelligent and prominent men and women to her card evenings, among them Horace Walpole, who came from across the square and pretended to complain about her entertainments. Perhaps he came chiefly for the morsels of court gossip, but he may also have been drawn by Kent's astonishing architecture;

ABOVE The first-floor Saloon rises through two storeys.

RIGHT Kent's coffered ceiling has scenes of amorous activities.

for even he admitted that at No. 44 the architect had created 'as beautiful a piece of scenery and, considering the space, of art, as can be imagined'. The outside of the house is of noble plainness, good-quality brickwork with stone dressings, and the rather masculine rusticated front door surround is the only emphasis.

William Kent, painter, garden designer and architect, is seen here at the top of his powers. He was engaged upon building two town houses at the time, this one and another in Arlington Street for the Prime Minister, Henry Pelham (see page 46). Lady Bel got the better house and friendship clearly blossomed: when the architect died, he left her four busts in his will.

Kent was no doubt instructed to provide one spectacular room for entertainments and a grand staircase to convey the visitors to it. With no requirement for more than one main bedroom, he could concentrate on the Saloon. Kent produced a room that rises through two floors, so that externally the second-floor windows are blind. He brilliantly coffered the ceiling to blunt the loftiness, with Roman Renaissance-style interlaced painted lozenges, hexagons and square grisaille against red and blue. A close examination of the subject matter reveals sexual activity. Today the Saloon is covered in mauve damask enlivened by a glittering border of gilt and glass. It is a room straight out of a Hogarth painting.

If the Saloon is one of the grandest eighteenth-century rooms in London, Kent unleashed his greatest imaginative powers on the staircase, a space of the utmost fantasy. Starting as a single stair, it divides into two arms and at that point the visitor becomes aware of the soaring composition with its apsidal, columnar screen of Ionic columns. Only Robert Adam's staircase at Home House (see page 100) comes near it for concentrated brilliance. The *trompe l'œil* effect of the cascading staircase is reminiscent of Italian baroque stage scenery.

After Lady Bel's death the house was acquired by the 1st Earl of Clermont, whose name has attached to it ever since. The Clermonts were a racing family and he was known as Father of the Turf. He won the Derby with Aimwell. Horace Walpole was still crossing the square for dinner and had not lost his feline touch when, one evening in his presence, Lord Clermont declared that he had read that it was Scipio who first introduced the toothpick from Spain. Walpole recorded: 'I did not know so much, nor that his Lordship ever did read, or know, that Scipio was anybody but a racehorse.' Henry Holland, the Prince Regent's architect, redecorated the bedroom and boudoir *circa* 1790 in a chic Frenchified manner.

No. 44 Berkeley Square was to be a childless house. The Clermonts left it to their nephew, who sold it to Charles Baring Wall MP. The 4th Marquess of Bath briefly owned it, followed by Sir Philip Burrell, MP, before it passed to the Clark family. It remained a private house occupied by Charles Damer Clark until 1959. The house was rescued by John Aspinall – an eighteenth-century throwback if ever there was one – who created the Clermont Club. He brought in the architect Philip Jebb and the greatest decorator of the age, John Fowler, and together they restored the house with panache and created the Gothic Pavilion in the former garden in the spirit of the Royal Pavilion at Brighton. The basement where Lady Bel's entertainments were prepared is now Annabel's club. No. 44 has remained at the heart of London gossip.

ABOVE Henry Holland decorated the bedroom and boudoir in the Louis XVI manner.
RIGHT The Gothic Pavilion, created by Philip Jebb and John Fowler 1963–64 for club use.

THE HOUSE OF ST BARNABAS

1 GREEK STREET

I first became aware of the House of St Barnabas as I walked through Soho on a winter's evening. In the twilight, the Georgian corner house proclaimed itself as the mistress of Soho Square. The lights blazed out from upstairs windows and through them I could glimpse exquisite rococo ceilings. Curiosity was aroused and I wondered who had lived and worked there? The answer would be surprising anywhere except Soho: slave owners, Tractarians, engineers and philanthropists. It was the office of the first metropolitan authority for the city and from here the sewers and a more salubrious London were planned. Charles Dickens introduced the house into *A Tale of Two Cities.*

'Of all quarters in the queer adventurous amalgam called London,' wrote John Galsworthy in *The Forsyte Saga*, Soho 'dwells remote from the British Body Politic.' At the turn of the eighteenth century Soho had aristocratic ambitions,

but it was to be an area of idiosyncratic development, a place of entertainment and carnal delights, the raffish buffer zone between the grandeur of Mayfair and the markets of Covent Garden. The area was characterized by waves of immigrants: Huguenots, Greeks, Irish, Italians and Jews. The lungs of Soho have always been its eponymous square and here on the corner with Greek Street lies the House of St Barnabas.

Like so many houses in London, 1 Greek Street was a speculation, built between 1744 and 1746 by a bricklayer, Joseph Pearce, but left undecorated within. Externally it is plain, with darkened brick, and rather old-fashioned for its date. Richard Beckford acquired the house in 1754 and it was almost certainly he who commissioned the exuberant rococo interiors. Compared to his brother Alderman William Beckford (later Lord Mayor) and his nephew the collector William Beckford, Richard is a shadowy figure,

RIGHT Richard Beckford's swagger staircase, by an unknown architect.

but his fortune derived from the same slave plantations in Jamaica that produced the most profitable commodity of the time, sugar.

The interiors are much as Beckford left them and are among the finest surviving examples of the rococo in London. Their architect is unknown and was probably a talented craftsman working in the manner of Isaac Ware. The staircase might belong to a rich merchant's house in Bristol or York. It is the first-floor drawing room which is the showpiece of the house. A Palladian-style chimneypiece, overmantel and panelling are crowned with a ceiling in an exuberant rococo style more common in Dublin than London. The central oval medallion shows putti in the clouds holding the symbols of the four elements. There are several other rooms decorated in a similar hybrid Palladian/ rococo style and to the same quality.

In 1755 Beckford left London and his trustees sold the house the following year for £6,300 to Sir James Colesbrooke, who lived there until his death in 1761. His executors sold it at a loss for £4,000, a demonstration of the declining fortunes of Soho. Several owners came and went until in 1811 the house became the offices for the Westminster Commissioners of Sewers. Beckford's bedroom became Sir Joseph Bazalgette's office, which still bears his name today, and it was here that he worked on the construction of the sewers. His importance in the story of nineteenth-century public works in London can hardly be overemphasized. The Commissioners mutated into the Metropolitan Board of Works in 1855; as the first authority of its kind in London, this may be viewed as the first seed of the office of the London mayor.

In 1861 the house was sold for £6,400 to the House of Charity, who have been there ever since. Founded in 1846 to help homeless and destitute women, the charity was a product of the Oxford Movement and intended 'to offer to those who are sunk in the depths of temporal, and frequently spiritual, wretchedness, the example of the discipline of a Christian family'. The building was renamed the House of St Barnabas after the apostle who showed kindness to others. It was a well-connected charity that only lacked a place of

OPPOSITE AND LEFT In the first-floor drawing room exuberant rococo plasterwork jostles with a Palladian chimneypiece and overmantel.

worship. In 1862 Mrs Gladstone laid the foundation stone of the magnificent and wholly unexpected Gothic revival chapel in the garden at the back of the house. This richly decorated building of French inspiration was designed by Joseph Clarke and illustrates the style of the Anglo-Catholic revival and the Tractarians. The chapel's opulence did not come cheap, and three original eighteenth-century chimneypieces were sold for £350 to help the costs. Today the chimneypiece in the drawing room is a copy made around 1962.

The garden, which despite the incursion of the chapel is still large by London standards, has been identified as the model for that belonging to Dr Manette and Lucy in *A Tale of Two Cities*, 'a cool spot, staid but cheerful, a wonderful place

for echoes, and a very harbour from the raging streets [with] a courtyard, where a plane tree rustled its green leaves'. The tree is still there today.

In the twenty-first century the charity continues to fulfil its noble purpose of helping the homeless. Today the house is used to raise money with, among other things, a private members' club buzzing with life, a place full of contemporary art, bars and meeting rooms. No. 1 Greek Street and its garden have always been, as Dickens observed, an oasis in the hurly-burly of Soho. The house has seen many occupants and functions that reflect the changing face of the district. The present use as a meeting place for entertainment and philanthropy continues that tradition.

ABOVE The Bazalgette Room was once Sir Joseph's office. Here a more salubrious London was planned.

ABOVE RIGHT Overlooking Soho Square.
BELOW RIGHT The unexpected High Victorian chapel.

THE MANSION HOUSE

THE CITY

At the heart of the City of London, where seven arteries converge, lie the Stock Exchange, the Bank of England and the Mansion House. The last is the official residence of the Lord Mayor. The Mansion House was built between 1739 and 1752 as a backdrop for the civic, ceremonial and convivial obligations of the office and has remained the symbol of the power and wealth of the City ever since. A piece of architecture by George Dance the Elder, it is far from perfect: it lacks grace and proportion. Yet its sturdy magnificence and robust detail give the house an energy entirely suitable to its position and purpose.

The office of Lord Mayor is first mentioned in 1189. The Lord Mayor is elected annually from the ranks of City aldermen. The election takes place on Michaelmas and the year in office follows a time-honoured pattern of shows, banquets and functions. Within the City walls only the

sovereign has precedence over the Lord Mayor. The need for a permanent residence was first mooted after the Great Fire of London in 1666 but nothing was done until the 1730s, when the practice of lodging the Lord Mayor in one of the City halls was becoming inconvenient to all parties. A small group of architects was approached to submit designs. Since George Dance was in the process of being appointed Clerk of the Works to the City of London and his two main rivals, Giacomo Leoni and James Gibbs, were Roman Catholic, the result was probably a foregone conclusion.

The chosen site of the new house was awkward and, although seemingly quite large, it was not large enough for the apparent needs of office, so Dance was forced to build upwards. The result, with an imposing giant hexastyle Corinthian portico facing the front, has always been a little top-heavy. The original entrance hall through the portico (now offices) introduces

LEFT The City's arms, supported by a pair of plump cherubs, preside over the vestibule of the Mansion House.

us to the main themes of the house: elaborate plasterwork, statues, and ornamental overdoors with cherubs holding armorial escutcheons. In the nineteenth century the main entrance was moved to the side elevation and visitors today come up the modest west staircase to the principal floor.

The Mansion House consists of a surprisingly small number of enormous rooms. The first of these, the work of George Dance the Younger, is the Saloon, whose main feature is eight fluted Doric columns that divide the room into three. The Lord Mayor's office, known as the Venetian Parlour on account of its vast Venetian window, has the first of many outstanding chimneypieces, as well as elaborate plasterwork by George Fewkes. The Long Parlour, used for meetings and small lunches, is handsome but, like so much of the house, architecturally eclectic. The problem stems in part from the fact that Dance the Elder seems never to have been entirely sure in which style he was building – Wren, baroque or English Palladian.

The Egyptian Hall is the most resolved and successful room in the house and one of the great interiors of London.

TOP AND OPPOSITE The monumental scale of the Egyptian Hall grandly echoes Vitruvius.
ABOVE The Ballroom, or Dancing Gallery, on the second floor.
OVERLEAF Embellishments include Sir Richard Westmacott's statuary.

ALFRED THE GREAT.

Based on the idea of the Vitruvian Egyptian Hall, the room achieves a true Roman grandeur. The main elements are two rows of eight giant Corinthian columns, the coffered barrel-vaulted ceiling by Dance the Younger, the huge stained-glass windows (nineteenth century) and the walls lined with figures from English literature, including Comus, Hermione and Griselda (all nineteenth century). The principal floor is completed by two drawing rooms with Adam green walls that set off the crimson coverings of the Nile suite of furniture.

In the Ballroom, or Dancing Gallery, situated on the second floor, the delicate plaster trophies celebrate music, flirting and dancing. The private sitting room on the same floor is, with its Palladian-rococo plaster panelling, the only other room in the house that could be called feminine. Two bedrooms complete the parade of state rooms. Not everything of interest at the Mansion House, however, happened above ground. One of its unusual features derived from the house being one of the City's two magistrates' courts. The basement contained ten cells for men, and one for women (known as the 'birdcage'), where Emmeline Pankhurst was once detained.

It is striking how few memorials and portraits of previous lord mayors exist in the house today. The term of office was too short and the house does not dwell on its past occupants in the way that so many civic palaces do. If the Mansion House was not rich in paintings, this dramatically changed in 1987 when Lord Mayor Sir Robert Bellinger announced the gift to the Corporation of the City of London of the Harold Samuel Collection of eighty-four Dutch seventeenth-century paintings. This group was the finest of its kind assembled in Britain in the post-war era. The result is that such masterpieces as Frans Hals's *The Merry Lute Player* today greet the visitors on the stairs and one of the main features of the South Drawing Room is Philips Koninck's great *Panoramic Landscape*.

The Mansion House has always received a mixed press from architectural historians, who have tut-tutted about Dance's often clumsy throwing together of elements. Sir John Summerson tartly noted 'the building is a striking reminder that good taste was not a universal attribute in the eighteenth century and that in the City of the 1730s there was a great deal more money than discrimination.'[1] Well, perhaps, but the Mansion House has admirably served its purpose for over 250 years, and it is held in great affection by the City.

[1] John Summerson, *Georgian London*, London 1945, p. 47.

LEFT The South Drawing Room, with Lord Samuel's paintings and the Nile suite of furniture supplied in 1803 by John Phillips to celebrate Nelson's victory.

COVENTRY HOUSE

106 PICCADILLY

Coventry House, overlooking Green Park, is perhaps the handsomest house on Piccadilly. For most of its life it was a gentlemen's club, and through its doors passed all of fashionable London. Today it is the only house in Mayfair that can claim to be a university.

The fringes of Green Park were one of the most desirable locations in eighteenth-century London. This was particularly true of the east side, with its great parade of palaces. The north side of the park, on Piccadilly, was also home to several important houses, notably Burlington House (built in the 1660s) and Devonshire House (completed *circa* 1740), followed by Coventry House in 1761. The west end of the street was colonized in the nineteenth century by the Rothschilds, who owned several houses adjacent to Apsley House.

Coventry House, which was originally No. 29 Piccadilly and later became No. 106, was built in the Palladian style for Sir Hugh Hunloke, probably by Matthew Brettingham.

Hunloke never lived there and three years later, in 1764, he sold it to George, 6th Earl of Coventry, for £10,000. Lord Coventry was a colourful Worcestershire landowner who engaged Robert Adam to redesign Croome Court (1760–81). Despite disputes over the architect's bills, Lord Coventry also asked Adam to produce designs for his Piccadilly house. Today only the Great Chamber on the first floor has a glorious Adam ceiling: this is in coral and green against a cream background, with painted medallions by Antonio Zucchi. There is an exuberant design by Adam in the Soane Museum for the Countess's octagonal dressing room on the first floor. This may have been destroyed, but there is the tantalizing possibility of its survival under later decorations.

The 6th Earl of Coventry was surrounded by interesting women. In 1752 he married a notable Irish actress, Maria Gunning. The marriage was not a success (and the Earl embarked on an affair with the courtesan Kitty Fisher).

LEFT The ceiling of Adam's Great Chamber.

LEFT A corridor
created for the
St James's Club.

The Countess had a passion for make-up, which was not shared by her husband, who once publicly wiped it off her face. She died aged twenty-seven of lead poisoning from cosmetics. Lord Coventry then married the Hon. Barbara St John, the first Countess of Coventry to live in the house. She is said to have had a passage dug beneath Piccadilly to the Ranger's House in Green Park, but no trace of her burrowing has been found. Their son, the 7th Earl, brought in Thomas Cundy the Elder, who remodelled several rooms *circa* 1811 and put in the balcony. The house was sold, presumably by the 8th Earl, and became a raffish gaming house known as the Coventry House Club, which accepted lady members. Then, between 1860 and 1864, the house was the residence of the French Ambassador, Count Charles de Flahaut, a veteran of Waterloo who was an illegitimate son of Talleyrand.

In 1867 the St James's Club opened negotiations for the building and acquired a twenty-one-year lease. Their tenure, the longest in the history of Coventry House, lasted until 1975. The club was founded in 1859 when Earl Granville, tired of the long waiting lists at the Travellers' Club, canvassed the entire diplomatic corps in London, both British and foreign. The flavour of the club turned out to be aristocratic and diplomatic (it had an unusual number of foreign members for a London club), with a sprinkling of literary and artistic souls. When the 15th Duke of Norfolk joined the club in 1870 it confirmed another aspect of the membership, old Catholic families. Henry James went there as a guest in the 1870s to study 'English colloquialisms', although, given its exotic composition,

one member thought you would be lucky to hear English spoken at all.

The club's artistic credentials in the twentieth century were impressive. Augustus John was a member, as were the two Osberts, Lancaster and Sitwell, and Terence Rattigan. Anthony Powell may have based the character of the young Widmerpool on a member, Denis Cuthbert Capel-Dunn.[1] The German Ambassador Joachim von Ribbentrop joined in 1937 and while everybody else in London found Hitler's envoy insufferable, the club butler described him as 'such a nice gentleman'.[2] Evelyn Waugh became a member in 1939, reputedly to give himself a refuge when Randolph Churchill was at White's, and Ian Fleming spent part of the war living at the club.

The club was not graced with great paintings until 1922, when the Society of Dilettanti deposited its matchless collection of portraits by George Knapton and Sir Joshua Reynolds on loan. 'The nominal qualification' for the Dilettanti, according to Horace Walpole, 'is having been in Italy and the real one being drunk.' The two great club portraits by Reynolds hung majestically in the coffee room, formerly the Great Chamber, on the first floor. The club rooms were painted either dark green or red, colours suggested by Osbert Lancaster, apparently on the advice of the artist John Piper.

By the 1960s the world of grand diplomacy was fading and with it one of the main supports of the club. The club acquired a reputation for backgammon, attracting players such as Lord Lucan and Alan Clark, but this was not enough to stem the decline in membership. By 1975 the St James's was in severe financial difficulties (not helped by living on a lease) and the club amalgamated with Brooks's. In 1977 the building was taken over by a language institute who renamed it International House. A decade later, the building became Limkokwing University of Creative Technology, which was formally opened by the Malaysian Prime Minister in 2007. The university and its students enjoy the building today.

[1] Desmond Seward, 'The St James's Club', in Philip Zeigler and Desmond Seward, *Brooks's: A Social History*, London 1991, pp. 125–26. When somebody challenged Anthony Powell with this suggestion, he merely said 'Seward is a clever fellow.'
[2] Ibid., p. 126.

LEFT Matthew Brettingham's original staircase.
ABOVE The Dilettanti portraits, while hanging in the St James's Club.

3 GRAFTON STREET

MAYFAIR

No. 3 Grafton Street reflects three ages of great wealth in London: the Georgian boom, the Edwardian swansong of great private houses, and the first decade of the new millennium, when international wealth poured into the capital to save its crumbling fabric. Today the house is a company office, but it has made the adaptation with panache.

Grafton Street is a short L-shaped street in the heart of the West End which contains a small, distinguished group of Georgian houses. The parcel of land on which it was built passed from Charles I to the Corporation of London in 1628 to cover a debt. The Earl of Clarendon leased it to extend his garden when he created his great palace on Piccadilly, Clarendon House. As so often in London development, it was the end of the lease that allowed the development of Grafton Street in its present form from 1765 onwards. The 3rd Duke of Grafton was the principal figure and Robert Taylor was his

architect. Taylor was popular with developers because, as *The Oracle* for 20 January 1792 wrote, 'Sir Robert Taylor . . . would erect you an elegant habitation, he would furnish it as you pleased – deliver in the tradesmen's bills more reasonably than you could contract for, and he charged a single *Five* per Cent. for his trouble.'[1] The result is, externally, a series of noble plain houses with fine classical doorcases which, as Marcus Binney pointed out, have the look of eighteenth-century Dublin.

The Duke and the architect, acting as speculators, produced some of the grandest terraced houses in London on an awkward site which followed the boundary of the Conduit Mead (meadow) and Aybrook stream. Here Taylor made clever use of a long narrowing site, terminating the house at the back in a five-storey octagon, with one octagonal

[1] See Richard Garnier, 'Grafton Street, Mayfair', *The Georgian Group Journal*, vol. XIII, 2003, p. 250.

RIGHT Edwardian imperialism: the staircase hall by Fairfax B. Wade.

room on each floor. This gave a view on to the south end of Berkeley Square and the garden of Lansdowne House (until the twentieth century obliterated this sylvan outlook).

The first resident of 3 Grafton Street was Admiral Howe, whose successful naval career included the victory of the Glorious First of June over the French (1794) and quelling the mutiny at Spithead in 1797. He lived in the house from 1767 until his death in 1799, by which time he had been created the 1st Earl Howe. His beautiful wife, Mary, is remembered for being the sitter for one of Gainsborough's most graceful portraits, now at Kenwood. Lord and Lady Howe would still recognize much of the house, particularly the ground floor with Taylor's lovely ceilings. The pilastered dining room has one of the best of them, a glorious Palmyra ceiling of octagons and medallions.

Despite the long tenure of Lord and Lady Dungannon, from 1814 to 1873, the nineteenth century saw several owners of No. 3, including James du Pré (shades of A.A. Milne?). The Dungannons' colourful neighbour at 4 Grafton Street was Henry, Lord Brougham, the founder of Cannes. Georges Augustus Cavendish-Bentnick occupied No. 3 from 1874 and it was his younger daughter, Mary Venetia, who married Arthur James, to whom the lease of house was transferred in 1891. The James family, although British, were wealthy from an American fortune. Arthur's nephew was the surrealist patron Edward James.

Arthur James covered 3 Grafton Street with a rich Edwardian sauce of marble and panelling. Perhaps surprisingly, this overlay did not destroy the delicate quality of Taylor's work but enriched it. James's architect was Fairfax B. Wade, whose most theatrical effect was blasting through the staircase landing to create an unforgettable *trompe l'œil*. Wade coated the hall and approaches with rich orange marble. If opulence is the main accent on the way up, the big first-floor saloon speaks of Edwardian comfort. A huge white-panelled room whose walls leave no space for paintings, it might easily be the setting of one of Oscar Wilde's plays.

ABOVE Gainsborough's ravishing portrait of *Mary, Countess Howe*, c.1760.
RIGHT The ceiling of one of the rooms in Taylor's octagon. The decoration is later, but follows his octagonal plan.

ABOVE Taylor's staircase overlaid by Wade.

OPPOSITE The Louis style of the saloon reflects a transatlantic taste.

The ceiling contains a large circular Venetian canvas by Giambattista Crosato which suitably depicts *Abundance Crowned by Fame while Minerva Repels Avarice*.

The James family occupied No. 3 until 1948, when the house was plunged into post-war uncertainty. Helena Rubinstein had her upscale beauty salon there between 1953 and 1971, and I remember my mother disappearing there during my childhood. A Greek bank followed, until the purchase by the present owner, who restored the house, giving it a postmodern twist with Italian contemporary furniture. Donald Insall Associates were the architects and did an excellent job.

SPENCER HOUSE

ST JAMES'S PLACE

Spencer House is the queen of London houses. Grand and graceful, it contains many of the most beautiful mid-eighteenth-century rooms in the capital. From the moment it was built Spencer House stood at the centre of perhaps the most brilliant society England ever produced, the Whig aristocracy that steered the country's fortunes in the second half of the eighteenth century. Few families were richer or more artistic than the Spencers, who built the house, lived there until 1926, and still own the freehold. In 1985 the house was rescued by Lord Rothschild, who undertook a heroic restoration and refurnished the house as it was in its eighteenth-century heyday.

Prodigiously rich, John Spencer, later 1st Earl, inherited a collection of pictures from his great-grandmother, Sarah, Duchess of Marlborough, but had no suitable London house. In 1755 he commissioned the Palladian architect John Vardy to build a house on a prime location overlooking Green Park.

However, following the discoveries of Herculaneum and the new interest in ancient Greek architecture, Lord Spencer began to seek something more up to date. It was probably Colonel George Gray, a fellow member of the Society of Dilettanti, who advised and oversaw the transition from the pleasing Palladianism of Vardy to the hyper-elegance of James 'Athenian' Stuart's neoclassical interiors. Stuart was at the forefront of the new movement, co-author of *The Antiquities of Athens* and the obvious candidate for such a job.

Georgiana, Lady Spencer, a famous beauty, was a partner in the creation of the house and much of the classical iconography it contains was a celebration of their blissful union. While she cut 'a very pretty figure' in society, Lord Spencer was a shy man of whom Lord Palmerston said 'the bright side of his character appears in private and the dark side in public'.[1] The building of Spencer House was the great achievement

[1] Joseph Friedman, *Spencer House*, London 1993, p. 38.

LEFT John Vardy's garden front overlooks Green Park.

of their lives, taking eleven years (1755–66). In the interval they went on the Grand Tour and collected even more works of art. Lord Spencer had a penchant for large seventeenth-century Italian 'wall-fillers', which were balanced by the enchanting series of family portraits he commissioned from his friend Sir Joshua Reynolds.

On completion Spencer House was recognized as a prodigy, and it attracted the most brilliant society. The ubiquitous Horace Walpole was of course a regular, and so, more surprisingly, was Laurence Sterne. Visitors approached

the house via St James's Street and were greeted by Vardy's rusticated entrance. The handsome and dignified external elevations are all by Vardy. Internally, the architect never got beyond the ground floor.

The grandest of Vardy's rooms is the Dining Room, in pale green broken by two columnar screens. Vardy designed the spectacular Kentian tables (Henry Holland removed these when he redecorated the room for the 2nd Earl, but Lord Rothschild persuaded the present owners, the Victoria & Albert Museum and Temple Newsham, to lend them back). Vardy's *pièce de*

résistance, however, is the Palm Room beyond, a cocktail of palm trees and classical forms, the most exotic creation of Georgian London. Both Vardy and his successor, Stuart, were steeped in classical ornament, which gave authority to their work; but, the source of the Palm Room is an unexecuted design by Webb for Charles II's bedchamber at Greenwich Palace.

Sometime in 1758 Lord Spencer gave Vardy the devastating news that Stuart would be completing the first-floor parade of rooms. Stuart had returned to England in 1755 and after eight years in Rome and four in Greece, his authority was

BELOW LEFT The Dining Room, by Vardy.
BELOW RIGHT The climax of the ground floor is the exotic Palm Room, Vardy's masterpiece.

ABOVE LEFT Vardy's original tables, as reinstated by Lord Rothschild.
ABOVE RIGHT An inventive detail: 'S' for Spencer on the door handles.
OPPOSITE 'Athenian' Stuart's Great Room, the centrepiece of the house.

absolute. Marred by soaring estimates, delays and Stuart's alcoholism, the relationship between architect and patron was not to be a happy one. However, the results justified the pain. The Great Room, which occupies the central position on the first floor, is the grandest surviving room of its date in London. With a high coffered ceiling, it is twice the height of any other room in the house. The detail may be Greek but the impression is of Roman richness. Nowhere has the Rothschild restoration more effectively replaced missing items, with brilliantly copied pier tables, mirrors and doors, and the hanging of appropriate paintings. In 2010 Guercino's *King David*, recently acquired at auction, returned to its original position.

Stuart reserved his most ingenious effects for the Painted Room, which, like the Palm Room below it, comes at the end of the parade. Here he pulled out all the stops to create a room decorated with *grotteschi* and roundels featuring Hymen, Venus and Cupid that drew upon many sources – Herculaneum, Raphael and Ancient Rome. It is the first integrated neoclassical interior in Europe and the precursor of the fashion for Etruscan rooms. At some point in the nineteenth century the original cream background was changed to a warmer green, which subsequent occupants have seen no reason to alter.

Each generation of the Spencers has added its own touches to the house. The 2nd Earl Spencer, the greatest of book collectors, brought in Henry Holland, who not only altered

the Dining Room but turned the Palm Room into a library. During the nineteenth century the house welcomed kings, queens, celebrities and geniuses. It was on the very short list of London houses that Queen Victoria thought suitable for the Prince of Wales to visit. But by the 1880s, with the collapse of agricultural rents, the Spencers were forced to search for tenants for Spencer House.

The most colourful tenant was the cockney millionaire Barney Barnato, known as 'the Great Barnato'. He took a lease in 1895 and commented, 'It's not a bad position. Exactly halfway between the Prince of Wales in Marlborough House and the PM in Arlington Street.' He filled the house with a raffish mix of bookies, impresarios, boxers, rabbis and actors. When Barnato once gave a courtroom his address, the puzzled judge asked if he was Lord Spencer's major-domo. 'No,' Barnato replied, 'I'm my own bloody domo.'

The last Spencer to live in the house was the 7th Earl, 'Jack' Spencer, known as 'the Curator Earl' for his interest in the family treasures. He restored Spencer House and furnished it in the sparse taste of the 1920s. By 1926 the house was let again, to the Ladies' Army and Navy Club, who were in occupation at the outbreak of World War II. Lord Spencer had already removed the contents, and with the coming of the Blitz he took doors, chimneypieces and anything movable to Althorp, the family's country seat. When, in May 1941, a bomb fell on Bridgewater House next door (see page 164), it shattered the south and west front windows of Spencer House and weakened the structure.

Post-war, Spencer House looked doomed. Nearly every other great London house had been sold and demolished. Christie's briefly used it between 1948 and 1956 and a succession of leaseholders came and went. It was the appearance of Lord Rothschild that transformed the position. His office was next door and members of his family lived in the street. The plight of Spencer House both moved and intrigued him. As he later wrote: 'Gradually a plan emerged: if the Trustees . . . would grant us a long lease and if Westminster Council would agree to give planning permission in perpetuity for office use, then the "planning gain" could be invested in restoring the State Rooms to their former glory.'[2] This is exactly what happened.

The team Lord Rothschild assembled was stellar and too large to describe. David Mlinaric was chief decorator and Dick Reid chief carver. Suffice to say that it would have been easier to rebuild the house from scratch, such was the complexity of squaring commercial and office needs with a fastidious

[2] Joseph Friedman, *Spencer House*, London 1993, p. 7.

restoration. Fittings were brilliantly replaced, and contents begged, borrowed and bought. Only somebody with Lord Rothschild's influence, determination and corporate power could have achieved the most impressive restoration project in 1980s London. Today Spencer House looks and feels like the house the 1st and 2nd Earls Spencer knew. A great work of art has been restored to full beauty. The historian Edwin Beresford Chancellor in 1908 said of the Painted Room that 'it is truly a room in which to dream about the past'. Today that could be said of the whole house.

OPPOSITE Stuart's Painted Room: the first neoclassical room in Europe.
ABOVE 'My own bloody domo', Barney Barnato.

20 ST JAMES'S SQUARE

ST JAMES'S

Behind the enlarged facade of 20 St James's Square lies a virtually intact suite of Robert Adam interiors showing the architect at the top of his form. The house was built for a pleasure-loving Welsh baronet, Sir Watkin Williams Wynn, 'the Welsh Maecenas' (1749–1789), whose many enthusiasms included music, art collecting, theatre and Welsh history. He showed a conventional interest in racing, hunting, freemasonry and politics but there is no doubt that his heart lay with the arts. Adam provided him with a worthy setting where he could display the treasures he acquired on his Grand Tour and could entertain his fellow members of the Society of Dilettanti to musical soirées.

St James's is the most venerable of London squares[1] and its creation marks the beginning of the development of the West End as we know it today. St James's Palace had been there since Tudor times, but the laying out of the square and the streets radiating from it took place between 1660 and 1690. It was the brainchild of the Earl of St Albans, who acquired the lease from the Crown and then implored Charles II to grant him the freehold in order that his clients would 'build palaces'.[2] The King agreed, and the Earl proposed three or four stately palaces on each side. The Great Plague delayed matters until the Fire of London made building plots in the West End so desirable that the number of houses in the square was increased to twenty-two.

The original house at No. 20 is rather a mystery, but by 1771/2 it was described as 'very ancient and much out of repair'[3] when Lord Bathurst sold it for £18,500 to Sir Watkin Williams Wynn, 4th Baronet, for demolition. He initially

[1] Not the earliest; that was Bloomsbury Square and Covent Garden for the Earl of Bedford.

[2] See Introduction.
[3] *Survey of London*: vol. 39, *The Grosvenor Estate in Mayfair*, Part I (General History), London 1977, p. 164.

RIGHT Adam's dazzling geometry in the upper level of the staircase hall.

RIGHT A copy of
Raphael's *Transfiguration*
forms the focus of
Adam's scheme.

asked James Gandon to draw up plans but, like many others before him, Sir Watkin was seduced by the dazzling talents of Robert Adam and changed horses.

Robert Adam returned from an extended Grand Tour in 1758 and swept all before him. Over the next decade he worked on remodelling or completing a series of country houses: Harewood, Croome, Compton Verney, Kedleston, Bowood, Osterley and Syon. His London houses begin with Lansdowne House in 1765 but date mainly from the 1770s; he designed 20 St James's Square in 1772–73. Why were patrons like Sir Watkin content to sack their existing architect in favour of the Scotsman?

Let us for a minute examine Sir Watkin Williams Wynn. He was one of the richest landowners in Wales, with 100,000 acres – although never quite rich enough for his ambitions. He inherited when he was five months old and went on an extravagant Grand Tour in 1768–69. In Rome he sat for his portrait to Batoni and commissioned paintings from Gavin Hamilton and Anton Raphael Mengs. Sir Watkin's connections with the leading artists and antiquaries in Rome no doubt sealed his artistic interests. Robert Adam was at the centre of this world, a gentleman architect who had absorbed all the latest archaeological discoveries as well as the fashionable currents of French neoclassicism. Adam provided his clients with plans for a parade of rooms that offered extraordinary variety, ingenuity of plan, brilliant colour schemes and fluidity within an overall scheme. This is what Sir Watkin was given at No. 20.

Of the outside of the house Adam wrote, 'It is not in a space of forty-six feet, which is the whole extent of the elevation, that an architect can make a great display of talent. Where variety and grandeur in composition cannot be obtained we must be satisfied with a justness of proposition and elegance of style.' Adam was competing with 'Athenian' Stuart's facade at 15 St James's Square. He produced a solution that was almost perfect, until the facade was compromised by a twentieth-century rebuild.

Internally the house has miraculously survived, and it is well maintained today as the headquarters of a software company. The hall, simple and elegant, has roundels with the trophies of war, and a lead plaque giving the date of the work. The ground-floor front room, the Eating Room, with columns and a Palmyra ceiling, leads to the Music Room. Music was Sir Watkin's great passion, particularly the work of Handel, whose manuscripts he collected. He would give musical breakfasts and himself played the violoncello. Adam provided an elaborate scheme of plasterwork panels enlivened with painted scenes

by Antonio Zucchi of shepherds and nymphs doing homage to the ashes of Handel and Corelli. Originally the panels on either side of the chimneypiece held commissioned paintings, *St Cecilia* by Reynolds and *Orpheus* by Dance; these were removed by a later baronet. The famous organ Adam designed for this room is now in the National Museum of Wales, along with other furnishings from the house.

The staircase was always too narrow for its height, giving a rather lofty feel. An exquisite copper stair rail takes the visitor up to the first floor, where Adam provides the visual tricks to overcome the awkward proportions, a large apse under a semi-dome with three niches. The semicircular arcading is continued around the staircase to frame a copy of Raphael's *Transfiguration* on the opposite wall. Looking up

ABOVE Adam's original facade, before it was duplicated in the twentieth century.

RIGHT The Rear
Drawing Room, with its
painted vaulted ceiling.
OPPOSITE The scin-
tillating ceiling of Lady
Wynn's Dressing Room.

the staircase to the second floor and the roof, Adam breaks up the space with a gallery of arches and pilasters surmounted by an oval skylight.

The first floor is notable for its extraordinary ceilings. The simplest is in the Front Drawing Room, where the main interest is Adam's chimneypieces after Piranesi. The anteroom overlooking the square, today called the Queen Mother's Room, has a cross-vault ceiling, but the most dazzling ceiling is that in Lady Wynn's Dressing Room. Here Adam solves the disadvantage of a narrow high room with a groined ceiling resting on two barrel vaults and a giant Palladian window. The finest room in the house, however, is the Rear Drawing Room, with its apsidal ends and astonishing vaulted ceiling where plasterwork and painted panels are in perfect harmony. One of the reasons for Adam's success was the close attention he gave to the synthesis of carpets, furniture, mirrors and fittings and mercifully some of these are surviving in the room, albeit later copies.

The Wynn family occupied the house until 1906, when they leased it to the Queen Mother's father, the Earl of Strathmore. While she was not brought up in the house, she would have known it well. In 1920 the Wynns sold the

freehold to the Eagle Star Insurance Company, who in turn sold it to the Distillers Company in 1935. Distillers also acquired No. 21 and the following year the architects of the Ritz, Mewes and Davies, blended the two facades and added the cumbersome top-storey mansard. The proportions of Adam's facade were lost.

In 2009 Mike Lynch, an IT mogul with a Cambridge mathematics background, acquired the lease of 21 St James's Square. Needing more space for his company, Autonomy, he added No. 20 as an afterthought. Fortunately, he is proud and protective of No. 20 and realizes that the house gives his organization a distinctive and unexpected profile for a software company. On my visit to inspect it I was left alone in the Rear Drawing Room to make notes and I reflected on the accurate words of John Summerson, 'The rooms in an Adam house are not a simple aggregate of well-proportioned and convenient boxes, but a harmony of spaces – a harmony in which many contrasts reside. The hall, the staircase, each room, each closet, fits into a counter-point of living-space; each wall has been caressed in the architect's mind.'[4]

---

[4] John Summerson, *Georgian London*, London 1945, pp. 126–7.

HOME HOUSE

PORTMAN SQUARE

Home House is Robert Adam's surviving London master-piece. Here the Scottish architect was determined to show his superiority to James Wyatt, and he produced a dazzling set of rooms that trumped his rival. Built for the 'Queen of Hell', the house has a raffish history with respectable interludes, notably under the greatest of all British collectors of Impressionist paintings, Samuel Courtauld. It was in this house that he established the art history institute that bears his name. An early director was Anthony Blunt, the so-called Fourth Man, who lived in the house and held risqué parties there. Today it is a fashionable club.

Elizabeth, Countess of Home, was by all accounts unattractive, but she was very rich. She snared the feckless 8th Earl of Home, who married her in 1742 only to abandon her two years later. Her fortune derived from Jamaica and she lived in a demi-monde world of West Indian connections; it was they who dubbed her 'Queen of Hell'. She was renting a house in Portman Square when, at the age of sixty-eight (already twice widowed), she acquired a nintey-nine-year lease on 'a parcel of ground' on the north side of the square. Lady Home engaged James Wyatt as her architect, fresh from his triumph at the Pantheon in Oxford Street.[1] He did not, however, give his client the attention she desired and in January 1775, when the shell of the building was already roofed and rated, she replaced him with Robert Adam. As Eileen Harris has written, 'The competitive urgency elicited the highest degree of Adam's artistic imagination. He was at his best when confronted by such a challenge.'[2] To rub salt in the wound of his competitor, Adam demolished Wyatt's staircase to produce one of his most perfect creations.

[1] Burnt down in 1792 but the architectural wonder of the time.
[2] Eileen Harris, *The Genius of Robert Adam: His Interiors*, New Haven and London 2001, p. 300.

LEFT Adam's finest London staircase.

LEFT Adam and neo-Adam: Philip Tilden, working for Lord Islington, added decorations to Adam's original scheme. ABOVE The staircase provides a brilliant example of Adam's skill in resolving internal space.

The hall at Home House is simple. It sets the tone with an apsidal fireplace and demonstrates Adam's passion for symmetry with no fewer than three false doors. The appearance of the staircase, equalled in brilliance only by Kent's at 44 Berkeley Square (see page 54), is breathtaking. Adam ingeniously uses the ovaloid space to wrap the staircase in a rising embrace, taking the eye up and around the first- floor recessed arches, culminating in an upper columnar gallery surmounted by a dome and skylight. Today's yellow marbling and painted statues of Minerva and Juno are early twentieth-century embellishments, attractive in themselves but not the austere stone effect with tripod lamps that Adam designed.

The stairs lead to an anteroom, which Wyatt had already finished. Adam turned all his guns on the Music Room, an architectural jewel box where everything is in motion. As this was a room of entertainment, Adam allowed himself some fantasy. It is the poetic product of the compass, a symphony of circles, niches and lunettes. Adam formed an inner shell in order to create deep window apses echoing arches on the chimney wall. The circular theme is picked up on the ceiling like a musical clockwork pattern. The walls have pilasters and glass panels, although the focus was originally an organ, removed in the nineteenth century. It is Wyatt's Pantheon in small.

William Beckford – a fellow West Indian – has left behind an account of a zany musical evening at the house in 1782 which gives the flavour of the Countess. One morning she picked up a couple of buskers, 'tall, athletic Negros in flaming laced jackets, tooting away on the French horn – "by God" exclaimed her [infernal] majesty . . . "you shall perform tonight at my concern" '. Her 'Maestro di Capella' was less than enchanted, complaining, 'I doubt whether they play in score, persons of that sort seldom do.' She insisted they stay and Beckford, more amused than impressed, made laudatory noises. 'There,' said the Countess, turning round triumphantly to the rueful maestro, 'did I not tell you so? Mr Beckford is a real judge.'[3]

The Great Drawing Room contains a superb chimneypiece with inlaid coloured scagliola and the best ceiling in the house. The room was altered in the nineteenth century, and Adam revival wall decorations were added. The first-floor parade of rooms comes to an arresting completion with the Etruscan Room, a square room which Adam declared 'differs from anything hitherto practiced in Europe' (which was not, however, entirely true).

Downstairs is a little muted after the glories upstairs. The Front Parlour is a masculine room enlivened by four dark red marble columns against grey walls and grisaille scenes from the *Aeneid* painted by Zucchi. Among the main ornamental features of the house are Zucchi's ceiling and wall panels, so delicate and appropriate, with Virgilian themes and muses. The Dining Room has them in abundance.

[3] Ibid., pp. 303–4.

Adam's main problem here was height and he uses pilasters to create an upward thrust in an otherwise long, low room. The Library has the main concentration of Zucchi's panels, broadly celebrating the triumph of wisdom, and in particular British wisdom, with cameos of national poets and philosophers.

It is usually stated that the history of Home House after the infernal Countess was uneventful, but this is far from true. The Marquis de la Luzerne lived there when French Ambassador (1788–91); he was a wily diplomat who had passionately supported the cause of America against Britain.

OPPOSITE AND ABOVE The Music Room, with Adam's musical clockwork pattern.

ABOVE The Etruscan Room: the finest of its kind in London.
OPPOSITE Adam used pilasters to raise the height of the
Dining Room. Alan Dodd's recent panel painting was done
for the club.

The stormiest period for Home House was that of the
occupation of the 4th Duke of Newcastle (1820–61), a hard-
nut reactionary and manic depressive who stirred up anti-
Catholic feeling, evicted tenants on political grounds and
vehemently opposed the Reform Bill. The mob revenged
him by stoning Home House and burning down one of his
other houses, Nottingham Castle. In contrast, Sir Francis
Goldsmid campaigned for the abolition of Jewish disabilities

from the house during his occupation 1862–1919. He was followed by Lord and Lady Islington, who prettified the staircase.

The twentieth-century giant was Samuel Courtauld, who brought with him the greatest collection of Impressionist paintings ever formed in Britain. A hard-working textile manufacturer, he was austere in everything except art. He sensitively restored Home House and displayed his astonishing collection around the rooms: Manet and Renoir in the Music Room, Cézanne in the Great Drawing Room, Seurat and Cézanne in the Front Parlour and more Cézanne and Manet in the Dining Room. When Courtauld's wife died in 1931 he set up the first institute dedicated to art history in Britain; this took over the house, while the collection eventually moved to a separate gallery at Woburn Square.

The aim of the Courtauld Institute was to teach art from 'the pyramids to Picasso'. The building quickly became institutionalized, with green paint in the corridors, metal bookcases obscuring the Music Room and a tea room in the basement. The deputy director, Johannes Wilde, sequestered the Etruscan Room and an air of mild eccentricity pervaded the building. One of the earliest lecturers, Anthony Blunt, became director in 1947, with a flat on the second floor where he was to live until retirement in 1974. Blunt's flat was Spartan and cold but sported a painting by Poussin and an etching by Picasso. After 7 p.m. on weekdays and at weekends the building was closed to students and staff and it became Blunt's private house. The flat became the background for homosexual 'rough trade' parties, a considerable risk in those days, especially given Blunt's preference for guardsmen. He was sensationally unmasked in 1979 as the notorious Fourth Man of the Cambridge spy circle.

The Courtauld Institute remained at Portman Square until 1989, when it moved to Somerset House, and five years later the building re-emerged as a private members' club. The new owners completed a brilliant restoration of the house which involved reinstating missing wall paintings. With a new audience, the pronunciation of Home House changed. Previously, Home rhymed with 'doom'; today it rhymes with 'dome'. The infernal Countess has her final revenge on her renegade husband.

OPPOSITE The Front Parlour, with Zucchi paintings.
ABOVE The Triumph of Wisdom, as painted by Zucchi, is the overall theme of the Library.

STRATFORD HOUSE

11 STRATFORD PLACE

A nobleman's residence, an embassy, an auction house, an office, a picture gallery and now a clubhouse – Stratford House has played nearly every role available to a great London house. Although enlarged and rebuilt, it is in essence an eighteenth-century palace that is, unusually, the focus of a composition at the head of a cul-de-sac. The supporting buildings may have lost some of their elegance, but Stratford Place remains a pool of tranquillity that flows into the rushing tide of Oxford Street.

In 1795, the Revd Daniel Lysons wrote, in the *Environs of London*, of the splendid new mansions of Marylebone: 'The most remarkable of these, being all detached buildings, are Manchester House, Harcourt House, Foley-house, Chandos House, the Earl of Aldborough's at the end of Stratford Place . . .'[1] The last referred to was our mansion, created by the Hon. Edward Stratford, the son of an Irish peer, the 1st Earl of Aldborough. He acquired the lease in 1771 on a watery site over the springs of the Tyburn river from the City Corporation. Stratford was probably his own architect, and over the next decade, assisted by a young Irish architect, Richard Edwin, he produced a handsome house in the Adam style. Such an arrangement between a noble amateur and a young professional was fairly common in the eighteenth century. Lansdowne House was most likely their model.

Edward succeeded his father as 2nd Earl of Aldborough in 1777, and the house changed its name accordingly. The new Earl was in constant financial hardship and it was only a second marriage to Miss Elizabeth Henniker, who had a £50,000 fortune, that enabled the house to be completed. Its appearance then can be chiselled out of today's facade. The house originally had only five bays flanked by two

[1] Ronald Lightbown, *An Architect Earl: Edward Augustus Stratford*, London 2008, p. 96.

RIGHT Lord Derby's mirrored staircase by Romaine-Walker.

LEFT The Oriental Club's elephant.
RIGHT The club hall.

colonnaded wings that embraced Stratford Place. This composition was announced at the Oxford Street end by a pair of lodges surmounted by lions; one remains. An unusual feature of Stratford House was the Earl's private theatre, designed by William Capon and removed in 1784 when the Earl was forced to let the house for financial reasons.

Aldborough died childless in 1801 and the house temporarily passed out of the family. It had several grand residents who rarely stayed very long, including the Earl of Jersey, and notably the 6th Duke of St Albans, who lent the house to two Habsburg archdukes, John and Louis, and changed the name to St Albans House. Prince Paul Esterhazy, a Hungarian grandee, lived there while his new Austrian embassy, Chandos House, was being prepared. Not everyone was impressed by these continentals. Lady Harriet Granville dined at the house in 1816 and wrote to her sister: 'We dined there on Sunday. It was a dinner quite unrivalled in the records of dullness. The archdukes scarcely utter . . . they are as bored as they look . . . Esterhazy crowned this flow of soul. He is silly and tiresome to the supremest degree.'[2] When the Habsburgs left, a Romanov moved in: the Grand Duke Nicholas, brother of Tsar Alexander I.

By 1819 the lease had reverted to the heirs of Lord Aldborough, the Wingfield-Stratford family, who occupied

the house for a decade. They were followed by a succession of unremarkable tenants until the arrival of an attractive Irish family, the Leslies of Castle Leslie, County Monaghan, who entertained fashionable and artistic London. Disraeli came, climbed the staircase and exclaimed 'What perspective!' Jack Leslie was Winston Churchill's uncle by marriage and one day introduced Winston to his childhood hero, Rider Haggard. The family produced a fine writer, Sir Shane Leslie, Bt, who described the house as 'the unhygienic palace built by Lord Aldborough'.[3] The Tyburn had become an open sewer and the house was notorious for its pong. Shane Leslie recorded an epigram about the house which refers to a related problem:

Possessed of one fine stair of state
It holds no closet nearer than the gate;
The foods and wines you cannot count
But there's no Jakes for guests to mount!

When the Leslies ran out of money they passed the house to their son-in-law, Walter Murray Guthrie, who employed Rosa Lewis as his cook. In 1902 Stratford House was acquired by Sir Edward Colebrooke, who created one of its most successful rooms, the rich panelled library. His tenure

[2] Hugh Riches, *A History of the Oriental Club*, London, 1988, p. 104.

[3] Ronald Lightbown, *An Architect Earl: Edward Augustus Stratford*, London 2008, p. 86.

was only six years. After that it was taken over by one of the wealthiest members of the nobility, the Earl of Derby.

The house, renamed Derby House, reached its zenith during this time. The 17th Earl abandoned his home in St James's Square and in 1908 commissioned the fashionable firm Romaine-Walker and Jenkins to rebuild the Stratford Place house. They enlarged and refaced the facade, created a new Louis XVI mirrored staircase, and brought in fixtures and fittings from Lord Derby's other houses, notably The Oaks in Surrey. The grandest addition was the enormous ballroom built out the back (the last of its kind in London) in a Roman baroque manner. Perhaps more importantly, they fixed the drains.

The ballroom came into its own for a 1911 coronation ball which included eight imperial highnesses and thirty-two royal highnesses. Probably the most momentous occasion at the house, however, came five years later in the middle of World War I. On the morning of 5 December 1916

Lord Derby gave breakfast to Winston Churchill, David Lloyd George, Andrew Bonar Law and Edward Carson; this breakfast resulted in the Cabinet resignation of Derby and Lloyd George, which in turn forced the resignation of the Prime Minister, Asquith.

Between the wars, when aristocrats began the retreat to their country houses, Lord Derby maintained the house because, in his own words, 'Well, Lady Derby must have somewhere to change when she comes up from Coworth to go to the play.' With the coming of World War II he emptied the house, and he invited Christie's, the auctioneers, to take refuge there when their King Street premises was bombed. Lord Derby sold the house in 1946 and shortly afterwards the publisher Walter Hutchinson moved not only his office but also his extraordinary collection of sporting art into the house, whose name reverted once more to Stratford House. The art collection was opened to the public in 1949 as the National Gallery of British Sports and Pastimes, a venture

OPPOSITE Lord Derby's lost ballroom.
RIGHT Fame, with her trumpet, supports the fireplace by Thomas Banks.
BELOW The drawing room, with ceiling panels by Biagio Rebecca.

that failed after three years. The property was sold in 1955 and four years later the Oriental Club stepped in. The club bought the freehold, and has been there ever since.

The Oriental Club has a history stretching back to 1824. The Duke of Wellington, the club's first and only president, gave the founders two characteristic pieces of advice: 'Have a club of your own' and 'Buy the freehold'. The club has maintained a flavour of the East and as Thackeray (who mentioned the club in *Vanity Fair*) observed, it has always prided itself on its anonymity. It remains one of the most discreet London clubs.

Today the house, as refaced by Lord Derby, is handsome and the interiors for the most part are pleasant essays in the Adam manner. The finest first-floor room, the drawing room, has a ceiling by Biagio Rebecca and an exceptional fireplace attributed to Thomas Banks showing Fame and Mars, with the Muses in relief. The greatest surprise on this floor is a rococo smoking room with painted panels of scenes of *galants*. The best room on the ground floor is unquestionably Colebrooke's library, a warm, luscious 'Adam' panelled room in cherry and gold. Sadly, the club rebuilt the ballroom as two floors of bedrooms, but in every other respect its arrival has saved Stratford House.

LEFT AND ABOVE Sir Edward Colebrooke's library: Edwardian neo-Adam of superb quality.

DOVER HOUSE

WHITEHALL

The British genius for the picturesque is seen nowhere to greater advantage than at Horse Guards Parade. The composition of William Kent's buildings, St James's Park, the Admiralty and Gilbert Scott's Foreign Office has a satisfying informality at the heart of government. In one corner stands Dover House, elegantly unobtrusive, a link between Horse Guards and the Cabinet Office. It is the least known of great London palaces – which, given its flamboyant occupants, is strange. Today it is the headquarters of the Scotland Office.

Dover House lies on the edge of Henry VIII's Tiltyard, part of the vast Whitehall palace complex. Between 1755 and 1758, Sir Matthew Featherstonhaugh acquired a fifty-year lease and commissioned the Palladian architect James Paine to build a new house set back from Whitehall, aligned with the Horse Guards building and overlooking the parade ground. Sir Matthew's widow sold the house for 12,000 guineas in 1787 to Prince Frederick, Duke of York, aged twenty-four.

The Duke had just returned from six years of travel on the Continent. He was George III's second son, the most useful and agreeable of a rotten bunch. A heavy gambler, the Duke was an able army administrator, if not quite so able a commander (as the nursery rhyme recalls). He was close to his elder brother, the Prince of Wales, and he invited the Prince's architect, Henry Holland, the darling of the Whigs, to make some alterations to the house. Holland filled in the Whitehall courtyard with a neoclassical rotunda incorporating a staircase to Paine's house. He presented a new facade to Whitehall, a rusticated screen broken by detached columns supporting the entablature and an Ionic portico, a composition showing Holland's up-to-the-minute appreciation of both ancient Greek and modern French architecture.

LEFT James Paine's facade for Dover House is to the right, overlooking Horse Guards Parade. It contrasts with Holland's Whitehall screen (shown above).

Holland also decorated a private suite of rooms on the ground floor for the Duke. However, the young royal was soon restless and on 29 August 1791 he wrote to his elder brother from Berlin, 'You know I always have longed for Melbourne House, which from its size and the capabilities of improving it, would be infinitely preferable for me, and I should be infinitely obliged to you if you would try if possible to persuade Lord Melbourne to part with it.'[1] This was exactly the kind of commission the Prince of Wales enjoyed and a month later he was able to report that he had been over the matter with Lord Melbourne and Henry Holland and that with a financial contribution to cover the fact that Melbourne House[2] was a freehold as against the Duke's leasehold, an exchange could be arranged. Inevitably, it turned out to be more complicated.

Lord and Lady Melbourne moved to Dover House in early 1793. They belonged to that charmed circle of Whig families who ruled England for most of the eighteenth century. Their heir, the Hon. William Lamb, married the beautiful Lady Caroline Ponsonby in 1805 and they were allocated the first-floor rooms of the new Melbourne House; this was to be the theatre of their very public existence at the epicentre of the Whig social milieu. Lord David Cecil described their life: 'Here, attended by a retinue of pages in liveries of scarlet and sepia designed by Caroline, they kept open house; received morning and afternoon visitors, gave dinner parties lasting till one in the morning after which the guests would sometimes descend to Lady Melbourne's apartments on the ground floor for supper.'[3]

At first the marriage was blissful. But Caroline was ruled by passion and saw herself as a romantic heroine. While her husband pursued his ultimately successful political career, she was to make herself notorious. She cultivated men of letters and intellectuals and it was almost inevitable that she would fall for Lord Byron. 'That beautiful pale face will be my fate,' she famously exclaimed. Byron would pass the day in her room at Melbourne House, but it was their public behaviour that scandalized London. Her husband sought a

[1] Dorothy Stroud, *Henry Holland: His Life and Architecture*, London 1966, p. 193
[2] Which survives in Piccadilly as apartments; see page 13.
[3] David Cecil, *The Young Melbourne*, London 1939 (new edition 1954), p. 82.

LEFT AND ABOVE Holland's astonishing conception was to turn a staircase into a rotunda.

separation but did not go through with it. Lady Caroline died at the house in 1828, the same year that William succeeded his father as 2nd Viscount Melbourne.

For economic rather than sentimental reasons, Melbourne sold the house in 1830 and moved to South Street in Mayfair. The purchaser was George James Welbore Agar-Ellis who, on being created 1st Lord Dover a year later, changed the name of the house to its present appellation. Agar-Ellis was an art collector, one of the founders of the National Gallery, and a friend of Sir Thomas Lawrence, who painted his portrait. He hung mostly British contemporary art at Dover House, apart from works by Guardi and Bol. Lord Dover died at the house in 1833. It remained with his family until 1885, when the government took possession; since then it has been the office of the Secretary of State for Scotland.

Entering Holland's pedimented screen, the first surprise is the rotunda entrance hall. This space of extreme elegance is ringed by eight Doric columns supporting a broad entablature under a dome skylight. The stairs rise majestically through the columns to an anteroom with a plaster copy of Michelangelo's *Tondo*. The original was owned by Agar-Ellis's friend Sir George Beaumont. The first floor has the three largest rooms in the house, which overlook the parade ground. They are surprisingly plain and contain Holland fireplaces. The Great Eating Room, today the Secretary of State's Office, has a ceiling modified for Agar-Ellis, while the Drawing Room still has a Paine ceiling.

RIGHT The Drawing Room contains one of James Paine's few surviving ceilings. OPPOSITE The anteroom with a copy of Michelangelo's *Tondo.*

The great surprise of the house comes on the ground floor, where three rooms survive from the Duke of York's private suite decorated by Holland. These rooms retain their warm, pastel, Regency colours. The Library, with its columnar screen and elegant doors, is used by ministers of the devolved administration visiting from Edinburgh. Its neighbour, room 11G in Civil Service parlance, otherwise known as the Painted Room, is the finest in the house. It was painted by Holland's team of decorators under Biagio Rebecca, with *grotteschi* panels and grisaille putti. The walls are Adam green and the overdoors bear a ducal coronet over a field marshal's baton and a sceptre. A door leads outside into the pretty garden and on to the parade

ground. The stillness and untouched Regency atmosphere of the room at the centre of the Whitehall machine is a great wonder.

The future of Dover House has been the subject of speculation. Inevitably, a palace at the heart of Whitehall drawing glowing comparisons against Downing Street has attracted attention. Gladstone was offered it as an alternative to No. 10 but refused on the grounds that if he lived at Dover House he would be 'forced to receive'. With the establishment of the Scottish government at Holyrood, the National Trust eyed Dover House as a desirable London showpiece, but the Scotland Office has reasserted its desire to hold on to this Whitehall beauty.

ABOVE AND OPPOSITE A surprising survival: the Duke of York's private apartments, decorated by Holland and his team of painters.

SIR JOHN SOANE'S MUSEUM

LINCOLN'S INN FIELDS

Of all the houses of London, Sir John Soane's Museum is probably the best loved. There is nothing quite like it. Although the product of Regency England, it has a timeless quality. Steeped in antiquity, the museum is a place where ancient Rome and Georgian Britain meet on equal terms. The roots are classical but the manner is entirely English. Hogarth's mob rubs shoulders with the *Apollo Belvedere*. Soane collected ancient, mostly architectural, sculpture but also modern paintings by his Royal Academy colleagues. However, his house in Lincoln's Inn Fields is above all a showcase for his architecture, which was a restatement of the classical tradition. Soane saw himself in a direct line of descent from Egypt, Greece, Rome, Inigo Jones and William Kent. The house demonstrates his belief that, as he put it, 'architecture is the Queen of the Arts . . . Painting and Sculpture are her handmaids.' What began as a London

home was extended, initially, for his burgeoning office and art collection, and finally became his museum, monument and laboratory of ideas.

John Soane was born the son of a bricklayer in 1753 and at the age of fifteen entered the architectural office of George Dance the Younger. Dance taught him a sense of the poetry of architecture and the rudiments of a modern classical style. The Dances were very cultured, appreciative of music and the arts, and this rubbed off on the young Soane. He also spent six years, from 1772 to 1778, working with Henry Holland. But the defining experience of Soane's life was his trip to Italy between 1778 and 1780 on a Royal Academy scholarship. There he was taken up by the Earl-Bishop of Derry and met Piranesi. Although he was too poor to buy anything on this trip, his later collections were informed by Grand Tour tastes. On returning to England he set up

RIGHT Sir Richard Westmacott's original plaster model for his statue of *A Nymph Unclasping her Zone* (*c.*1828)
perches on the edge of the Nymph Recess, above a model of Soane's masterpiece, the Bank of England.

A NYMPH
BY SIR R. WESTMACOTT R.A. 1755-1836
FROM THE ORIGINAL AT CASTLE HOWARD.

BANK OF ENGLAND   SOUTH FRONT

his own practice and married Elizabeth Smith, an heiress through her uncle, George Wyatt. It was Wyatt's death in 1790 that enabled the couple to buy 12 Lincoln's Inn Fields and start collecting.

As Soane's career prospered so did his ambitions. He bought a country house, Pitzhanger Manor in Ealing, which for a time became the main focus of his collections. Soane fondly looked forward to his two sons carrying forward the torch of his profession. However, they turned out to be feckless and Soane's disappointment in his offspring was to have far-reaching consequences. He sold Pitzhanger (1810) and concentrated all his energies on making a home for his collections in Lincoln's Inn.

Soane had purchased No. 13 in 1808 and later he bought No. 14 as well. He spent the rest of his life rebuilding, rearranging and perfecting what became his hobby and obsession. If his children could not be relied upon, Soane would make his own terms with posterity. He left nothing to chance; guidebooks were produced (the second of these, the *Description*, first published in 1830, was updated in 1832 and 1835), endless inventories and accurate watercolours were made to provide

definitive installations and arrangements of works of art. Finally, he obtained a special Act of Parliament enabling him to leave his house to the nation as a museum, with the stipulation that nothing should be removed or added.

A narrow hall leads to the main room of the house, which functioned as both dining room and library and where Soane entertained. It is a masculine room of deep Pompeian red walls, leather chairs and mahogany bookcases, which underlines the fact that Lincoln's Inn is a bachelor house. Mrs Soane, understandably given the constant dust and dirt, removed herself frequently to Margate (and died in 1815). We are introduced to the main themes of the collection: stained glass, antique objects and English paintings, dominated by the brilliant portrait by Sir Thomas Lawrence of Soane himself. The architectural use of mirrors, niches, pendants and incised decoration is characteristic of the house, although Soane was to give every room a separate identity, each more astonishing than the last. He was to combine the sleek lines of Thomas Hope's Duchess Street house – the *non plus ultra* of Regency good taste – with the antiquarian drama of Horace Walpole's Strawberry Hill.

LEFT The curious lantern in the Picture Room combines classical motifs with a structure of Gothic, or possibly even Jacobean, inspiration.

ABOVE The Pompeiian Red Library Dining Room – the largest room in Sir John Soane's house-cum-museum – is lined with presses containing his valuable collection of architectural books.

The study, where Soane wrote letters, was a link room but it is also the first of several artistic shrines, in this case a collection of architectural fragments collected by Charles Heathcote Tatham on behalf of Henry Holland. From sculpture, the collection moves to painting and into the Picture Room, which at first glance appears to be a room dedicated to English art, containing as it does Hogarth's two great series *A Rake's Progress* and *An Election*. But beside these rollicking, rumbustious scenes of eighteenth-century England hang drawings by two of the great prophets of continental neoclassicism, Clérisseau and Piranesi.

The heart of the house, and its greatest surprise, is the area covered by three areas, the Crypt, the Colonnade and the Dome, which merge together over two floors and contain the greater part of the collection of antique fragments, statues and plaster casts. The Dome area, with its amazing assembly of gods, urns, fragments and men, is the most startling space in the house. Its centrepiece is the *Apollo Belvedere*, a cast once owned by Lord Burlington. The Crypt – a marmoreal space that produces the effect of a catacomb, reflecting Soane's interest in the romantic effect of buried architecture and the Temple of Death – is dominated by the sarcophagus of Seti I, which Soane acquired for £2,000 after the British Museum rejected it. Soane celebrated its arrival with a three-day party attended by Turner and Coleridge.

From the ancient world of gods, and sarcophagi, the Breakfast Room brings us back to Regency England. Soane conducted interviews in this room under the shallow dome and lantern. It is the most successful room in the house. Upstairs, passing a shrine to Shakespeare on the way, lie the Soane family drawing rooms, vivid yellow rooms which no doubt owe their comparative simplicity to Mrs Soane. Here is a portrait of her two boys by William Owen, and adjacent is Turner's *Admiral Van Tromp's Barge at the Entrance of the Texel, 1645*.

There are a great many other attractions: the contemporary British paintings, the Monk's Parlour, where Soane comes closest to Strawberry Hill, and, above all, the great hidden treasure of the museum, an enormous collection of architectural drawings, not only Soane's own office archive

RIGHT In the heart of the museum, Sir Francis Chantrey's 1829 bust of Sir John Soane surveys his creation. Encrusted with marbles and plaster casts, the Dome area evokes the courtyard of a Roman palace.

RIGHT Upstairs on the first floor, the sulphur-yellow South Drawing Room provides a respite from Soane's collectomania. OPPOSITE Cunningly lit, canopy-domed, and incorporating 122 circular convex mirrors, Soane's Breakfast Room is a miniature, domestic version of the imposing top-lit banking halls he devised at the Bank of England.

but drawings from the offices of Robert and James Adam and of his old master, George Dance.

Soane got his Act of Parliament in 1833 and two years later a touching scene took place in the house. The chief members of the architectural profession came to pay homage to Soane as the indisputable father of his profession. They read a letter to the bedridden architect from the Duke of Sussex, followed by a formal address, and presented him with a gold medal. Overcome with emotion, he asked his solicitor to reply, saying that he proposed there and then to endow a charity for distressed architects and their families. That evening a gathering and ball in his honour took place at the Freemasons' Hall – attended by Soane's bust by Sir Francis Chantrey, crowned

with laurel – which all present felt did justice to England's greatest living architect.

Soane died two years after this event, having secured the future of his house-cum-museum. He knew only too well the fickle nature of posterity and taste. He was right: by the end of the nineteenth century, 'the museum had become notoriously deserted and irrelevant.'[1] During the twentieth century, however, Soane was rediscovered, as an architectural deity to both traditionalists and modernists. He wanted his house to be an inspiration, both practical and poetic, and in this it must be judged a success. The magic of this house of curiosities is very much alive.

[1] Tim Knox, *Sir John Soane's Museum, London*, London 2009, p. 39.

APSLEY HOUSE

NO.1 LONDON

Marooned by traffic, Apsley House today stands as lonely and erect as the Duke of Wellington on the battlefield of Waterloo. The house is many things: a shrine to a military hero, a home, an art gallery and an authentic glimpse of a great nineteenth-century *hôtel particulier*. Above all, it retains the character of Wellington himself, who celebrated his victories here, defended the house from rioters, and made it a centre of fashion and the background of his tumultuous political life. The style of the house reflects the robust transition between the Regency and early Victorian.

Apsley House takes its name from the Apsley/Bathurst family. Robert Adam built it for them between 1771 and 1778 as the end house on Piccadilly. Little of that house survives, but the Piccadilly Drawing Room still has an Adam chimneypiece, ceiling and frieze. Lord Apsley's grandson, the 3rd Earl Bathurst, sold the house in 1807 for £16,000 to Wellington's eldest brother, Richard, Marquess Wellesley, just returned as Governor General of India. Wellington, flush from victory at Waterloo, gave his brother £40,000 for it in 1817. Parliament had voted him a large sum which it was expected would be spent on a country palace *à la* Blenheim, for which several designs were drawn up. Perhaps surprisingly, the Duke decided that Apsley House would be his main residence; he plumped for a relatively modest country house at Stratfield Saye.

The Duke of Wellington on display at Apsley House is the public face, the man who entertained his generals, arranged his trophies of war, and represented Britain's enhanced position in the world. We do not see his austere downstairs bedroom or enter his private study. Kitty, his neglected wife, barely makes an appearance. And the essential simplicity of the man is lost. The Duke's military career, on the other hand, can be read through Apsley House's treasures.

LEFT Sir Thomas Lawrence's flattering portrait of the 1st Duke of Wellington, who created Apsley House as his public monument.

The unpromising third son of an Irish earl, Arthur Wellesley was sent to Eton and the military academy at Angers in France. It was to his arch-rival Napoleon that he owed his career opportunities, first in India, then on the Spanish peninsula, and later in their final and only direct confrontation at Waterloo. It is fitting, therefore, that the most striking artefact in the house should be Canova's vast nude sculpture of Napoleon, which the British government surprisingly acquired from the French in 1816 for 66,000 francs and the Prince Regent presented to Wellington. It stands over-large in the stairwell. Even Napoleon thought it *trop athlétique*.

Upstairs the parade of entertaining rooms contains the Duke's large and varied picture collection. Left to himself the Duke enjoyed Dutch genre paintings, and he had a fine group by Jan Steen, Jan van der Heyden, Nicholas Maes and others. Apart from the many commemorative portraits of his military colleagues and allies at Apsley House, Wellington's contemporary art followed his genre tastes. The Piccadilly Drawing Room holds many of the Dutch paintings and his most expensive modern painting: Wilkie's cheering *Chelsea*

Pensioners Reading the Waterloo Despatches, for which he paid £1,260.

Wellington's hanging arrangements were rather eccentric to the modern eye, but he carried them off by force of personality. The re-hang today is not always felicitous, particularly in the Portico Drawing Room. The State Dining Room, by Benjamin Dean Wyatt in 1819, was the first of Wellington's additions, and it was in this room that he held the early Waterloo reunion banquets. It carries well the state portraits, mostly presented by the sitters themselves.

It was Wellington's spell as Prime Minister and his removal to Downing Street in 1828 that created the opportunity for the most ambitious rebuild of the house. Wyatt added the portico and provided the famous Waterloo Gallery, in the newly fashionable French revival style. Although the innovations were architecturally a success, Wellington was appalled by the cost and rowed with the architect. Wyatt had vastly exceeded his estimates by providing nice touches such as shutters with mirrors, but the Duke's fury could not be assuaged. He refused to meet Wyatt and left it to his friend Mrs Arbuthnot to supervise the finish.

ABOVE LEFT Canova's giant *Napoleon* dominates the staircase hall.
ABOVE RIGHT The Striped Drawing Room.

RIGHT The Piccadilly Drawing Room, the finest surviving Adam room in the house.

ABOVE AND RIGHT The Waterloo Gallery, which contains 165 paintings from the Spanish royal collection.

The result, as she pointed out, is spectacular; the Waterloo Gallery remains one of the grandest rooms in London.

The annual Waterloo banquets were transferred to the gallery on its completion. Although referred to as the Waterloo Gallery ever since, it is equally a monument to the Duke's victories in the Peninsular War, because it contains most of his 165 important paintings from the Spanish royal collection. The group had been looted by Joseph Bonaparte and captured by Wellington after the Battle of Vitoria in 1813. The Duke attempted to return them to the King of Spain, who graciously told him to keep them. This princely haul of mostly Spanish works included four paintings by Velázquez and the Duke's favourite Italian picture, Correggio's *The*

Agony in the Garden. The last was glazed and only the Duke held the key of the glass, as he liked to dust it himself. He had a special hook in his carriage so that the painting could travel with him. The Duke hung the collection against yellow damask, to the despair of the architect, who thought it made nonsense of the gilding and was a bad background for the paintings. His descendants replaced it with more suitable red damask.

Apsley House was frequently attacked by the London mob during the Duke's political career, particularly when the Reform Bill was defeated in the Lords. He gave instructions that if a crowd collected they should be told that the house would be defended and they had better go

somewhere else; no one was to fire unless the gates were broken down.[1]

From the moment of the Duke's death in 1852, the house was recognized as a shrine or, as Mrs Arbuthnot had earlier put it, his 'Waterloo House'. The 2nd Duke opened the house to the public and created the present ground-floor Museum Room with mementoes, batons, dinner services and swords. Whereas nearly every other ducal family gave up their traditional London house between the two world wars, the Wellington family, aware of their special responsibilities, held on. It was the 7th Duke, an architect and antiquarian, who made the gift of Apsley House to the nation in 1947,

[1] Elizabeth Longford, *Wellington: Pillar of State*, London 1972, p. 234.

while retaining private rooms for the family. He undoubtedly saved the house by his public-spirited action. The Duke removed most of the family portraits to Stratfield Saye. Today it is the only great London house still to be inhabited by the family.

The house remained a part of Piccadilly until the widening of Park Lane in 1961–2 caused the demolition of its neighbours on the east side. Hyde Park Corner is the most unresolved of London spaces and the twentieth century has visited many vulgarities on the site, but Apsley House retains its dignity and rank as No. 1 London.

LEFT Victorious sovereigns grace the State Dining Room. RIGHT The Museum Room, with Wellington's memorabilia.

REGENT'S PARK VILLAS

MARYLEBONE

'Once and only once, has a great plan for London, affecting the development of the capital as a whole, been projected and carried to completion.'[1] Sir John Summerson was referring to the plan to cut a great highway through London from Carlton House on the Mall up to Marylebone (now Regent's) Park. Nash's elegant Regent Street has long since been rebuilt but the terraces around the park remain, and within their circumference lies a group of villas probably unique in any capital, each conforming to every picturesque notion of a country house in town.

The two principal movers in the great scheme were the Prince Regent and his architect, John Nash. Napoleon's Paris was a model. The great new thoroughfare through the heart of the capital would link the Regent's Carlton House with a royal pleasure dome or *guingette* to be created for him in the park. Originally over fifty villas were planned, in sylvan groves, to create a 'garden city' a hundred years before such things generally existed. After formidable obstacles which would have felled a lesser man, Nash succeeded in the main outline of the plan, although the buildings in the park itself were drastically modified. The Prince never got his *guingette* and the villas were reduced to eight, mostly in the north and west of the park, of which only four survive.

The Nash terraces are gloriously picturesque, throwing a girdle of creamy stucco stage scenery around the park, at its best seen from a distance.[2] This Arcadian classical dream land was the setting for the pleasant but surprisingly conservative villas that were to populate the park. They were mostly the product of the reliable talents of Decimus Burton.

[1] John Summerson, *Georgian London*, London 1945, p. 160.

[2] The cream colour is twentieth century. For most of the nineteenth century stucco was intended to imitate Portland stone.

RIGHT Nash's terraces frame Regent's Park.

OVERLEAF The Holme, probably the first villa in the park.

This solid practitioner of the Greek revival designed the Hyde Park screen, which John Betjeman thought was one of the noblest things in London, because it served no useful purpose.

Burton was only eighteen when he designed The Holme for his father, a successful speculative builder, in 1816–18. It was probably the first villa in the park, and it has the best site. Burton gave the stucco house a Corinthian portico and a dome which was later replaced with a balustrade. The Crown Lands Commissioners, who still own the freeholds in and around the park, complained, rather unfairly, that 'it is to be lamented for the beauty of the Park that Mr Burton was *allowed* to build the sort of house he has built.'[3] Several

3 J. Mordaunt Crook, 'The Villas of Regent's Park', *Country Life*, 4 July 1968, p. 24.

architects modified the house over the years but perhaps the most unexpected alteration was the Empire-style dining room by Stéphane Boudin of the great Parisian firm of decorators Jansen. The garden was largely the work of Geoffrey Jellicoe and, as is often pointed out, the view across the lake to the house is one of the finest picturesque set pieces in London. The Holme had many occupants, including the impresario Sir George Dance, and later the Departments of English and Italian at Bedford College, before reverting to private occupation (by the royal family of Brunei).

At the heart of Regent's Park lies the Italianate St John's Lodge, today in the – almost mandatory – cream stucco of the area. It had particularly noteworthy occupants. Originally built in 1817 by an obscure architect, John Raffield, for a radical MP, Charles Augustus Tulk, it was

modified by Burton for Wellington's elder brother, Lord Wellesley, in 1831–32. However, St John's Lodge owes its external appearance largely to Sir Charles Barry, who extended the wings with a ballroom and library and provided the loggia and entrance for the great Jewish philanthropist Sir Isaac Goldsmid. The most eccentric resident was the mystic Catholic convert the 3rd Marquess of Bute, who built more extraordinary houses than any other nineteenth-century aristocrat. At St John's Lodge Lord Bute contented himself with an internal makeover from 1892 by Robert Weir Schultz[4] in a vaguely Byzantine manner full of heraldic emblems, zodiacs and astrological symbols. Much of this decoration survives, as does Lord Bute's Garden of Meditation, which is now separated from

[4] Carried out by H.W. Lonsdale.

OPPOSITE Boudin's Empire dining room at The Holme.
ABOVE St John's Lodge, as extended by Barry.

the house. This unexpected refuge is open to the public and the quiet spirit of Lord Bute pervades this eye of the park. St John's Lodge briefly became the history faculty of Bedford College before reverting to private occupation.

On the north-west extremity of Regent's Park is Grove House. This house was built by Burton for George Greenough, the founder of the Geographical Society,

and it is the least altered. One of Greenough's successors, Sigismund Goetze, a once fashionable, now forgotten artist who painted the Foreign Office frescoes, added his own decorations to the main rooms; these were covered over in 1954 when the Nuffield Foundation acquired the lease. Perhaps the greatest surprise is the studio of Goetze, which survives as an enormous stand-alone building in the garden,

LEFT The hall of St John's Lodge, redesigned for the eccentric Lord Bute.
ABOVE RIGHT Grove House, the least altered of Decimus Burton's villas.
BELOW RIGHT The lost Goetze-painted room at Grove House.

today used as a concert hall. The house went back into private occupation when it was bought by the Australian Robert Holmes à Court, and is today the London home of the Sultan of Oman.

Clearly visible on the Outer Circle road is Hanover Lodge, approached through a pair of Greek Doric lodges and sporting a sumptuous entrance portico in the Erechtheion Ionic order. It was built 2006–9 for the Bagri family, from designs by Quinlan and Francis Terry, to replace a house probably by Burton. Though simpler and somewhat lifeless, this had anything but dull occupants. Built by the Peninsular war hero Colonel Sir Robert Arbuthnot, it was later occupied by the fiery sailor the 10th Earl of Dundonald, whom Napoleon dubbed 'Le Loup de Mer' and whose life was the stuff of legend. His successor at Hanover Lodge was his old adversary's elder brother, Joseph Bonaparte, in exile. The house seems to have attracted sailors, for in 1910 the future Earl Beatty, the hero of Jutland, moved in and asked Lutyens to make extensive alterations, which have mostly disappeared. Bedford College (once again) took the lease of Hanover Lodge from 1961 and built halls of residence on the land to the east between the road and the canal.

When the college left in 1995, the Crown Estate Commissioners offered a long lease of the building for adaptation as a private dwelling. In a bold gesture of patronage in 1988, the Crown Commissioners had allowed the strip of land to the east to become the site of six new villas. Each in a different, traditional idiom by Quinlan Terry, they are Ionic, Veneto, Gothick, Corinthian, Tuscan and Regency, and may be plainly viewed from the road but much more romantically from the towpath of the Regent's Canal on the other side.

Finally, in the same corner of the park, there is Winfield House, the residence of the American Ambassador to London.

ABOVE Hanover Lodge.
RIGHT Quinlan Terry's Ionic Villa (above) and Gothick Villa (below).

Among the many attractions of this house is the largest private garden in London (12 acres). Originally known as Hertford Villa, then St Dunstan's Villa, it was built by Burton for the devil's worst Regency rake, the 3rd Marquess of Hertford, known as the 'Caliph of Regent's Park', who used it for orgies. The house was damaged by fire in 1936 during Lord Rothermere's occupation. He sold it the following year to Barbara Hutton, the Woolworth heiress, who built on the site a large, neo-Georgian brick house with an eclectic interior, designed by Wimperis, Simpson and Guthrie. In December 1945 she offered the house to President Truman as the embassy residence. Ambassadors have come and gone – many hanging important art collections during their tenure – and Winfield House has been at the centre of London social life ever since.

Given the decline of the Regent's Park villas in the mid-twentieth century, it is extraordinary to think that today they are not only all returned to domestic ownership but also twice the number they were. A very pleasant walk may be had identifying them and capturing glimpses through trees and across water. Their occupants are fortunate to enjoy the finest *rus in urbe* that London can offer.

LEFT Winfield House, the residence of the American Ambassador.

LANCASTER HOUSE

STABLE YARD, ST JAMES'S

'In extent, grandeur of proportions, solidity of material and beauty of situation,' exclaimed the German visitor Dr Waagen, Stafford House 'excels every mansion in London.'[1] True enough, yet Lancaster House (formerly Stafford House) is too icily grand to be lovable. Once a palace for plutocratic dukes and now a show house for Foreign Office conferences and government hospitality, it boasts the grandest rooms ever created in London for private occupation. This house was for Britain's richest family in the world's richest city.

It began as a royal project. The Duke of York, whom we last encountered at Dover House, commissioned Robert Smirke to build a house on the prime site where Green Park intersects with the Mall. Under the influence of his mistress, the Duchess of Rutland, the Duke replaced Smirke with Benjamin Dean Wyatt, and thus began the long saga of

architects building on top of each other at Lancaster House. The house was only half completed when the Duke died in 1827, leaving behind a vast trail of debts. Enter George Leveson-Gower, 2nd Marquis of Stafford and later 1st Duke of Sutherland, who took on the lease and whose family successfully accumulated titles and fortunes to become the richest in Europe. This 'Leviathan of Wealth' – as Charles Greville described him – with a vast Midlands industrial fortune, married Elizabeth, Countess of Sutherland, who owned one million Highland acres in her own right.

The building of the house proceeded smoothly at first. The Marquis of Stafford resumed the work with Wyatt, who adopted the style contemporaries called Louis Quatorze, but was more accurately Tous les Louis. Stafford House was to become the greatest example of this genre. The cream and gold rooms are wonderfully elaborate, but the tour de force of the house was always the scagliola hall and staircase which

---

[1] Beresford Chancellor, *The Private Palaces of London, Past and Present*, London 1908, p. 348.

LEFT The scagliola-faced hall of Lancaster House: once the grandest private room in London.

ABOVE The lantern, with palm trees, designed by Barry in 1838.

RIGHT The Long Gallery, now lacking the great Sutherland collection of paintings.

had been completed four years before the (by then) Duke of Sutherland died in 1833. His successor, the 2nd Duke, wanted an additional storey added to the house and turned to Robert Smirke, who obliged, but this dissipated the dynamic of the design and rendered a box-like sterility to the exterior. It was rumblings of discontent about the unbusinesslike ways of Wyatt that had caused the family to use Smirke, whose merit was always to come in on budget. However, Wyatt was recalled to create the state apartments on the first floor, and it is to him that the main credit is given for the Frenchified interiors. The building process was managed by the family's estate manager, James Loch, later to become infamous for his part in the Highland Clearances. The uneasy collaboration between the architects was compounded when the 2nd Duke also brought in Sir Charles Barry, who worked on his country houses, Trentham, Cliveden and Dunrobin. Wyatt took the Duke to court and won, although he never found another patron.

London was astonished by the opulence of Stafford House. Although the Sutherlands were generally courtiers rather than politicians, the house immediately became a centre of fashion; it was described as 'the ballroom of London'. Disraeli introduced the house into *Lothair* as Crecy House and distinguished visitors to the capital were taken to Stafford House as a matter of course. Chopin played there, and Garibaldi stayed there on his 1864 visit to London. The 3rd Duchess gave a great ball in his honour, which upset both sides of the political divide. Both the 3rd and the 4th Duchesses were famous beauties and hostesses who opened the house so often to charitable functions that Beresford Chancellor thought that 'the interior of Stafford House is better known to the general public than that of any of the great Houses of London.'[2] Queen Victoria, although disapproving of the 3rd Duke, who, she thought, did not behave 'as a Duke should', was a close friend of the family and famously remarked to the 2nd Duchess, 'I come from my house to your palace.' A younger son of the 2nd Duke, Lord Ronald Leveson-Gower, wrote an enjoyable memoir about growing up in the house – and convincingly served as the model for Lord Henry Wotton in Oscar Wilde's *The Picture of Dorian Gray*.

The Sutherland reign at Stafford House ended in 1912 when the house was acquired by Sir William Lever, later

[2] Ibid., p. 347.

RIGHT The first-floor enfilade is the high point of the Anglo-French style in London.

1st Viscount Leverhulme, who renamed it after his native county. He bought it as a home for the Museum of London and a setting for government hospitality, and it is in the latter capacity that it survives today. The Museum of London decamped to Kensington Palace at the end of World War II. Lancaster House owes its preservation to Lord Leverhulme, its Crown freehold and its key position on the Mall.

In 1953 Sir Anthony Eden as Foreign Secretary hosted the coronation banquet in honour of the Queen at Lancaster House. The building gradually assumed its role as the background for government functions, and in particular, colonial independence negotiations. Perhaps the most famous of these was the Rhodesia conference under Lord Carrington in 1979.

Today the house has the detached grandeur of an embassy. Walking from the simple Ionic entrance hall into the staircase hall, we can only gasp – as President Mitterrand did – at the scale and richness. If the rest of the house is essentially white and gold, here all is rich, coloured marble and scagliola with huge copies of Veronese paintings. The main parade of state rooms is on the first floor. The Music Room and the Long Gallery represent the high point of the Anglo-French white and gold manner – only rivalled in scale by the Edwardian alterations to the Ballroom at Buckingham Palace. Of course what the house is lacking today is the art collection – never as great as that of Bridgewater House but nevertheless one of the wonders of London, with major works by Murillo, Veronese, Correggio, Delaroche and numerous Dutch masters. If the paintings have gone – to be replaced by the odd official portrait – the furniture and proliferation of giant gilt candelabra maintain the sense of opulence and no expense has been spared on curtains and wall hangings. The State Drawing Room in a restless rococo style and the Green Room are familiar as the setting for the 2010 film *The King's Speech*.

The ground floor holds another suite of semi-state rooms, the State Dining Room with red silk walls used for ministerial lunches, the Eagle Room and the Gold Room, any one of which would be at home in Compiègne or Schönbrunn Palace. This is the highly polished style of nineteenth-century royalty. Indeed, if Lancaster House lacks patina, it is because today it serves as the government extension to Buckingham Palace.

OPPOSITE The State Dining Room: despite government use, the house retains its decorative grandeur.
ABOVE The State Drawing Room: Benjamin Dean Wyatt's ceilings were of a richness unsurpassed in London houses.

BRIDGEWATER HOUSE

CLEVELAND ROW

Bridgewater House was London's nineteenth-century treasure house. It contained the greatest private collection of paintings assembled in Britain since the seventeenth century. Although the house boasted superb Dutch pictures, French furniture and a great library, it was the Italian and French pictures which enthralled visitors, the astonishing group of Raphaels, Titians and Poussins that remained there until, at the outbreak of World War II, they were moved to Scotland (where many of them have been on loan to the National Gallery ever since). Bridgewater House was built on a mighty scale in the Italian palazzo manner and is a statement of the wealth of the Egerton family, who at different times were Earls and Dukes of Bridgewater, Earls of Ellesmere and, later, Dukes of Sutherland.

Bridgewater House is approached diagonally along Cleveland Row, which, as is often pointed out, is a very small street for a very large house. The main rooms look out on to Green Park. The site was originally Berkshire House. Renamed Cleveland House, it was acquired at the very end of the seventeenth century by the 4th Earl of Bridgewater. His grandson, Francis Egerton, 3rd Duke of Bridgewater, was the key figure in the art collection. His life was devoted to creating the Manchester to Liverpool ship canal, which brought him an annual income of £80,000. The art collection he formed was a brilliant opportunistic response to the French Revolution, when the Duke was able to acquire the lion's share of the Italian and French paintings from the Orléans collection. He rebuilt the house to accommodate the paintings. His nephew and heir, who was, rather confusingly, Earl Gower, Marquis of Stafford and finally 1st Duke of Sutherland, was a partner in the so-called Orléans syndicate and with his additional collection found it necessary to create a new gallery in 1806 designed by Charles Heathcote Tatham. Since he already owned Stafford House

RIGHT The monumental Green Park facade by Barry.

(today Lancaster House) next door, he passed Cleveland House to his younger son, Francis Egerton, who was later (in 1846) created 1st Earl of Ellesmere. It was Francis Egerton who in 1841 commissioned the establishment architect Sir Charles Barry to create an Italianate palace in the manner of Sangallo's Palazzo Farnese in Rome. The design is essentially an enlarged version of Barry's Reform Club, with knobs on. It lacks the purity of the Reform but is certainly more ducal, with its monumental rusticated porte cochère and architectural ornaments.

Internally, the two main spaces were the Picture Gallery, which was destroyed in the Blitz, when, on the night of 10 May 1941, Bridgewater House took a direct hit; and the Marble Saloon (Hall), which survives. The Saloon rises the full height of the house, with a double arcade, one on top of the other. The first-floor open gallery held Poussin's *Seven Sacraments* series. The decoration of much of the interior, particularly the barrel-vaulted staircase, was entrusted by the 2nd Earl of Ellesmere to a German artist, Jakob Götzenberger, who worked in an Italian Renaissance idiom which so horrified Barry that he 'retired with deep regret'. Götzenberger's work, which has a Nazarene feel to it, was seen by some as luxurious and by others, including Barry, as debased.

The Picture Gallery, the work of Barry alone, was the main wonder of Bridgewater House. The collection of paintings had first been exhibited to an amazed London public at Bryan's gallery in Pall Mall in 1798, a quarter of a century before the foundation of the National Gallery. Barry designed the Bridgewater House Picture Gallery, with a public entrance in Little St James's Street, which opened in time for the 1851 Great Exhibition. The toplit gallery, broken at both ends with Corinthian columns, held over four hundred paintings, and visitors could enjoy such masterpieces as Titian's *Diana and Actaeon* and its pendant *Diana and Callisto*. The gallery was on the first floor, adjacent to the Dining Room and Drawing Room, both in the Louis XV manner, which happily survive. The Library, with its important collection of incunabula, and the Sitting Room,

OPPOSITE The porch on Cleveland Row, proudly dated 1849.

BELOW The lost Picture Gallery once held the cream of the Orléans collection of paintings.

which had held the three Bridgewater Raphaels, were on the ground floor and relatively little damaged.

The house was sold after the war to the Legal and General Assurance Company and has had many office occupants since then. To appreciate the massive, almost Piranesian, quality of Bridgewater House, walk around it on a winter's evening when the ornamental Victorian lamps are lit, enter the side street with the huge stucco service wing and there you will find the old disused door where the bell marked 'Picture Gallery' survives as a reminder of its former glory.

OPPOSITE ABOVE The Saloon rises the full height of the building.
OPPOSITE BELOW The Sitting Room once contained three Raphaels.
LEFT The marbled and painted staircase.
ABOVE The bell at the long-disused public entrance to the Picture Gallery.

SEAFORD HOUSE

BELGRAVE SQUARE

Seaford House is the grandest house in Belgravia. Rising behind iron railings on the corner of Belgrave Square, its plain stuccoed facade conceals a gorgeous interior of onyx halls and gilt drawing rooms. It was the home of peers until World War II, since when it has played host to the Imperial Defence College and its successor, the Royal College of Defence Studies.

The creation of Belgravia in the early nineteenth century was a successful piece of town planning that has remained astonishingly intact. It rose on the so-called Five Fields to become the grandest residential quarter of the capital. The architectural consistency and preservation of Belgravia are the result of the ownership being with one family, the Grosvenors, who became Marquesses and then Dukes of Westminster. The pivotal point of this elegant *quartier* remains Belgrave Square, named after a Cheshire village owned by the Grosvenor family.

Belgravia the golden
With mink and money blest . . .

From 1826 the Grosvenor Estates allowed the prince of Victorian builders, Thomas Cubitt, and three backers to develop the four terraces, using Soane's pupil George Basevi as their architect. They left the corners for stand-alone houses. Seaford House was built on the south-east corner in 1842 to designs by Philip Hardwick, the architect of old Euston Station. Externally the house is in the palazzo style of London clubs. It was initially called Sefton House after its earliest leaseholders, the 3rd and 4th Earls of Sefton. In 1902, the 8th Lord Howard de Walden acquired a forty-year lease, renamed it Seaford House (he was also Baron Seaford), and dramatically remodelled the interior with the architect J.J. Stevenson. The remodelling was luxurious and eclectic, much of it in Lord Howard de Walden's own antiquarian taste.

LEFT The opulent entrance hall.

Thomas Evelyn Scott-Ellis, Lord Howard de Walden (1880–1946) was an aristocratic dilettante whose fortune derived from the former estates of the Dukes of Portland in Marylebone. He had quite a bewildering number of interests, which encompassed music (particularly Wagner), theatre, fencing, falconry, motor boats and horse racing (in 1933 he won seventeen races). In addition he was a serious antiquarian and one of the editors of *The Complete Peerage*, but his main historical interest was focused on his Ellis Welsh roots. He became obsessed with the Mabinogion legends. Lord Howard even gave up renting Audley End as his country house and rented Chirk Castle in Denbighshire instead. In London, opera and theatre occupied his time and he himself wrote a number of librettos, plays and pantomimes. Given his romantic range of interests, Seaford House was a surprisingly conventional choice of London house, but no doubt its size appealed to him as a stage for concerts and theatricals. Among those who performed there were Toscanini, Paderewski and Sir Thomas Beecham.

Seaford House immediately reveals its most celebrated feature, the grandiose onyx hall and staircase, one of the most fabulous London interiors of its time. A legend has arisen that in order to ensure supply of the 42 tons required, Lord Howard de Walden bought a mine in South America. The entrance lobby with onyx columns leads up the stairs to a first-floor gallery supported by more onyx columns. Above this is an ingenious oval domed lantern supported by caryatids, by J.J. Stevenson.

LEFT The staircase is crowned by J.J. Stevenson's lantern.

The first floor contains the main reception rooms. They are mostly clad in cream and gold panelling dating from the 1840s. The largest of them, the anteroom, was given additional later decorations and has Frenchified painted scenes, showing Night, Dawn, Day and Evening. This was used by the Howard de Walden family as the ballroom. The dining room, now the lecture room, is from the 1902

OPPOSITE Legend has it that, to ensure the supply of onyx for Seaford House, Lord Howard de Walden bought an onyx mine in South America.
BELOW The first floor is mostly in the French style.

makeover: it has highly polished pilastered panelling in a heavy Renaissance manner and a gleaming white marble fireplace, giving a powerful impression of Edwardian luxury.

The ground floor throws up a couple of surprises that reflect the antiquarian interests of Lord Howard de Walden: the music room with painted beams, and his bedroom in a toy medieval castle style (he is plausibly said to have designed this himself). Perhaps the biggest surprise of all comes at the rear of the house, a large concealed courtyard with an octagonal clock tower like one at the back of a country house.

The house was requisitioned by the government in 1940 and it eventually took over the lease. A bomb destroyed the porte cochère, and its absence gives the house its rather flat appearance. In 1946 the Imperial Defence College moved into Seaford House, offering a strategic-level education on the defence of the British Empire. Its successor, the Royal College of Defence Studies, continues to inhabit the building today. Impossibly large for a private house, and even as an embassy residence, Seaford House continues to be maintained by the Ministry of Defence. A long roll call of distinguished visitors, from General Eisenhower onward, have lectured there.

ABOVE LEFT Hardwick's lobby on the first floor.
BELOW LEFT Lord Howard's whimsical historicism is evident on the ground floor.
RIGHT A rare survivor: the stable courtyard.

KENSINGTON PALACE GARDENS

Rich and sequestered, Kensington Palace Gardens is a world set apart. The grandest residential thoroughfare in London, the street is a stage for billionaires, potentates and embassies. The scale of the houses was always slightly preposterous and never matched by the gardens, giving them a passing resemblance to the summer cottages of Newport, Rhode Island. Indeed, there has always been something slightly un-English about these great whales set in a row. Their history is littered with exotic figures: foreign barons, bankrupt financiers, Randlords, the occasional aristocrat and some passable imitations of Bond villains.

It all began when a Treasury committee, appointed in 1838 to look into the royal gardens, decided to close down the kitchen gardens of Kensington Palace. Sir James Pennethorne provided a plan for a private street running between Kensington and Bayswater. In 1842 plots were offered on ninety-nine-year leases with stringent conditions attached. This was not, as the commissioners put it, 'attended with success', so when an entrepreneur, John Marriott Blashfield, appeared in 1843 and offered to erect twenty-one houses within five years, they felt compelled to accept. The commissioners wanted a minimum spend of £3,000 per house but Blashfield spent about £12,000 on each of the first five houses, which set the tone for the rest of the street but also led to his bankruptcy. Owen Jones was his architect and No. 24, with its onion domes and Moorish features, was typical of this phase. It was once the London home of the Maharajah of Baroda and is now, suitably, the residence of the Saudi Arabian ambassador.

Blashfield built the set of gates and the stucco lodge at the north end of the road, but by 1847 he had sold only two of his five houses and nine plots, not enough to save him.

RIGHT Owen Jones's No. 24 in the Moorish style, from the first phase of building.

The street looked doomed but limped through the 1840s. Its survival was largely thanks to the partnership of Thomas Grissell and Samuel Morton Peto, builders of the Houses of Parliament and Nelson's Column, who provided some of the finest houses in the street. By 1851 only one third of the street was occupied. The transformation in its fortunes was as sudden as it was unexpected. The Great Exhibition of 1851 helped to make Kensington more fashionable, while the growth of the town westward and the arrival of a prestigious tenant were all factors that caused every plot to be taken by 1854.

The early occupiers of the street were not particularly impressive, and the appearance of the 5th Earl of Harrington at No. 13 in 1851 was regarded as highly significant. He built what is probably the ugliest house in the street, a poor Gothic building, designed by Lord Harrington himself with C.J. Richardson, that is today the Russian Embassy. But Harrington was one of only a tiny number of British aristocrats who could be tempted out of Mayfair and Belgravia. Kensington Palace Gardens remained the preserve of the *nouveaux riches*. The fashionable world generally kept to the east end of the park and preferred to colonize Park Lane. As late as 1971 Mark Girouard could write that

Kensington Palace Gardens 'retains a curious atmosphere of not quite having made it, of not being altogether the genuine article'.[1]

The character of the street owes most to the Grissell-Peto partnership. Three of their houses in the Italianate manner, Nos. 12, 18 and 19, turned out in the long term to be among the most successful in the street. Peto himself moved into No. 12, which was designed by R.R. Banks, a pupil of Charles Barry, in the latter's Reform Club manner. Peto went on to make a colossal railway fortune and then lost everything. His successor at No. 12, Alexander Collier, a cotton merchant, had a Moorish-style billiard room created by M.D. Wyatt, which survives. Collier – in the spirit of the street, one is almost tempted to say – went bankrupt, and it was not until Lord and Lady Cholmondeley (Rocksavage at the time) moved in in 1920 that things looked up. They brought to No. 12 not only great works of art but also talented musicians as well as most of fashionable London. Legend has it that Sybil Cholmondeley – who lived in the street until 1971 – suggested to the French Ambassador that he move his residence there,

[1] Mark Girouard, 'Town Houses for the Wealthy: Kensington Palace Gardens I', *Country Life*, 11 November 1971, p. 1268.

PAGE 178
ABOVE The leafy tranquillity of 'Millionaires' Row'.
BELOW No. 20, with Nos. 18 and 19 beyond.
PAGE 179 Barry's double palazzo at Nos. 18 and 19 was recently united.

ABOVE LEFT Lord Harrington's arrival at No. 13 in 1851 raised the tone of the street.
ABOVE RIGHT No. 12 was the home of Lord and Lady Cholmondeley.
RIGHT The Moorish-style billiard room at No. 12 still survives.

which led to the new lease of life as 'Embassy Row'.[2] In fact the Russians were already there by 1930.

The largest and most splendid block in the street was Nos. 18–19, an Italianate pair designed by the office of Charles Barry. Peto's one-time partner, Grissell, moved into No. 19, but No. 18 had the more interesting residents. Baron Julius de Reuter, founder of the international news agency, occupied the house from 1868 until 1899. Viscount Lee of Fareham, who gave Chequers to the nation, lived there for five years from 1922, followed by the botanist/banker Lionel de Rothschild. By the 1970s, No. 18 was part of the Soviet Embassy, while the other half of the building, No. 19, was the Egyptian Consulate. In the early twenty-first century the houses were united for the first time by David Khalili and they are now occupied by a well-known Indian family. Only two of the four corner towers which make the house so distinctive are original; they lend a splendidly picturesque air to the composition.

One of the most distinguished houses in the street is No. 15, begun in 1854 by James Knowles for the rags-to-riches millionaire George Moore, who was shocked by his own vanity in possessing such a house. It became the scene of Christian missionary endeavour. Four hundred cab drivers were given dinner in the house and each presented with a copy of Bunyan. From 1937 the house was occupied by Sir Alfred Beit of the South African diamond family, who had inherited the fabulous art collection of his father, Sir Otto. He commissioned two fashionable architects, Lord Gerald Wellesley and Trenwith Wills, to design a rococo revival library, and a Palladian-rococo oval dining room to display the set of six Murillos of *The Parable of the Prodigal Son*. The rooms survive, but, alas, not with the contents, which were removed to Ireland. After the Beits, No. 15 became the Iraqi Embassy. It has now reverted to private occupation and is currently the subject of a major restoration. Beyond this the street turns into Palace Green, which was developed at the end of the nineteenth century.

The character of the street was always international. Figures such as Leopold Hirsch (No. 10), not to mention Reuter, Beit and Baroda, saw to that. By the 1980s the embassies had taken over but there are still enough privately owned houses for the street to maintain its other sobriquet of 'Millionaires' Row'. Uniformed guards monitor entrances and exits and today the experience of walking down Kensington Palace Gardens induces the melancholy that invariably hangs over the empty metropolitan houses of the very rich.

[2] Peter Stansky, *Sassoon*, New Haven 2003, p. 179.

OPPOSITE At No. 15 Wellesley and Wills designed a rococo revival library and Palladian-rococo oval dining room for Sir Alfred Beit. Both survive.
ABOVE The garden front in 2011.

DUDLEY HOUSE

100 PARK LANE

Dudley House is a rare Park Lane survivor. From the 1820s the world of fashion that clung so closely to Green Park extended itself along the eastern fringes of Hyde Park. Several great houses found a berth there: Grosvenor House, Dorchester House, Londonderry House – today all gone and replaced by luxury hotels. Dudley House, however, at the Oxford Street end, has not only survived but recently reverted to being a private residence, after sixty years of office occupation.

Park Lane began as an unlit track running behind the houses of Park Street. According to Harriet Wilson, the 3rd Marquess of Hertford used it for admitting prostitutes to his house. Grand houses had started to appear from the 1760s but improvements to the park during the nineteenth century, the removal of a high wall, the creation of Decimus Burton's Hyde Park screen and the desire for a verdant outlook were all factors in the making of Park Lane into a great address.

It is always said that the Ward family had associations with Dudley House as far back as 1737, when the lease was taken from the Grosvenor Estate by Anna Ward. She may or may not have been a relation of John, 6th Baron Ward, later 1st Viscount Dudley, who acquired the lease in 1756. The Wards were an old family who were reinvigorated at the beginning of the nineteenth century by vast coal reserves on their Staffordshire estates. It was the 4th Viscount who instigated a major rebuild of Dudley House in 1826.

Lord Ward was a minor politician who was created Earl of Dudley in 1827; he was known as 'the Lorenzo of the Black Country'. Contemporary reports about him differ. One court lady described Lord Dudley as 'a man who promised much, did little, and died mad'. Madame de Staël, on the other hand, thought he was 'the only man of sentiment whom she had

LEFT The dining room, designed by William Atkinson.

met in England'.[1] Dudley brought in as his architect William Atkinson, who provided him with the elegant ground-floor Ionic colonnade which now supports the cast-iron conservatory, the product of later improvements. Several of Atkinson's interiors survive, notably the dining room in a chaste Italianate manner.

Lord Dudley died childless in 1833 and after several grand tenants the house was occupied by the 11th Baron Ward. The family were at the zenith of their mining wealth in 1855 when Lord Ward commissioned Samuel Whitfield Daukes to transform not only Dudley House but also his vast country house, Witley Court in Worcestershire. In both cases the architect chose a heavily gilded Louis XVI style for the interiors. Daukes's most memorable rooms at Dudley House are the mirrored, chandeliered ballroom and the top-lit picture gallery, punctuated by columns of white Parian marble and scagliola.

When the new gallery was completed in 1858, Lord Ward filled it with his collection of Italian and Dutch paintings. The German art historian Gustav Waagen had seen the collection a few years earlier and admired Ward's taste for early Italian

pictures, which were becoming increasingly fashionable. He commented that 'Lord Ward permits access to his gallery, for cultivating this purer taste, while others may use the means thus offered for gradually acquiring it.'[2] Lord Ward hung two important Raphaels at Dudley House, *The Crucifixion* (now in the National Gallery) and *The Three Graces* (at Chantilly).

The Daukes improvements are evident in the exterior. He stuccoed the walls and added the conservatory to give Dudley House its present Park Lane appearance. The high point of the house was the state visit of the Khedive of Egypt in 1867. Lord Ward, by now Earl of Dudley (of the second creation), lent the Khedive the house, but regretted his generosity when he saw the damage his entourage caused. Dudley died in 1885 and his successor, the 2nd Earl, extended the conservatory over the whole front. He also started to sell the art collection.

By the 1890s Park Lane was enjoying its heyday of *nouveaux riches* arrivals, typically Alfred Beit, Ernest Cassel and Barney Barnato. Dudley House went the same way when the 2nd Earl sold the house in 1895 to the most unpopular of the so-called

[1] Edward Walford, 'Apsley House and Park Lane', *Old and New London*, vol. IV, 1878, pp. 359–75.

[2] Gustav Waagen, *Treasures of Art in Great Britain*, London 1854, vol. II, pp. 229–31.

Randlords, Sir Joseph Robinson, who had made his money from South African diamonds. Robinson filled the house with fashionable portraits by Gainsborough and Romney. Lady Dorothy Nevill remarked that the plutocratic collectors of the time surrounded themselves 'with the beautiful eighteenth-century portraits of the class they have conquered'.[3] Robinson hung Bouchers in the entrance hall and also had a large collection of Dutch and Italian paintings.

At a time when musical concerts were all the rage in London houses, Robinson gave grand entertainments at Dudley House, securing singers like Nellie Melba and Clara Butt. Lady Glover remembered one concert for 'a wonderful display of orchids and fairy lights, every delicacy in and out of season and the choicest wine'.[4] Even Sarah Bernhardt attended. But this did not help Robinson's poor reputation.

When Lloyd George suggested a peerage, George V refused outright, citing it as 'an insult to the Crown'.[5]

The Ward family, rather surprisingly, returned to Dudley House. The younger brother of the 2nd Earl, Sir John Hubert Ward, who married the daughter of the American Ambassador, acquired it in 1912 and lived there until 1938. Two years later Dudley House was badly damaged in the Blitz, and this might have been the end of the story. However, the Grosvenor Estate took the building back and in 1969–70 architects Basil Spence and Anthony Blee undertook a major office conversion which was sympathetic to the historic interiors. They even created a new classical upper hall with a coved ceiling.

Dudley House seemed destined to a future as an office. However, the house was sold in 2006 and at the time of writing (2011) is in the middle of a major renovation to restore it to domestic splendour.

[3] Lady Dorothy Nevill, *Reminiscences*, London 1906, p. 105; and Michael Stevenson, *Art and Aspirations: The Randlords*, South Africa 2002, p.140.
[4] J. Mordaunt Crook, *The Rise of the Nouveaux Riches*, London 1999, p. 183.

[5] Ibid.

OPPOSITE The conservatory was added in two phases in the nineteenth century.
ABOVE The ballroom, and the picture gallery, where Lord Ward hung his important collection of paintings.

THE SPEAKER'S HOUSE

THE PALACE OF WESTMINSTER

'May it please Your Majesty, I have neither eyes to see, nor tongue to speak in this place, but as the House is pleased to direct me, whose servant I am here.' With these famous words Speaker Lenthall rebuffed Charles I when he entered the Commons chamber in 1642. The Speaker's House is the visible symbol of the special position of his office as the guardian of the ancient privileges of the House and its representative. It reflects his status as First Commoner of the Realm and offers the finest suite of Gothic revival living rooms in London.

The first recorded Speaker was Sir Thomas Hungerford in 1377. The Speaker's position rose with the gradual ascendancy of Parliament over monarchy during the seventeeth and eighteenth centuries. The demands of office meant that by the end of the eighteenth century the Speaker was provided with accommodation in the precincts of the old Palace of Westminster. When the Duke of Newcastle,

the Auditor of the Exchequer, died in 1794, the Speaker took over his apartment and from then on the Speaker's House was a central feature of the palace. Speaker Addington moved in the following year and initiated the portrait collection of holders of the office which remains the dominant feature of the decoration of the Speaker's House. Every subsequent Speaker has had his portrait painted, even if posthumously. Addington's successor, Speaker Abbot, brought in James Wyatt to remodel the house at considerable expense, which, as *The Times* of 1805 reported, 'gives it entirely the air of a grand old dwelling'.

On the night of 16 October 1834 the Palace of Westminster dramatically burnt down, leaving Westminster Hall. The competition that followed specified that the new building should be in the Gothic or Elizabethan style. It was won by a classical architect, Charles Barry, who brought in the twenty-three-year-old Gothic firebrand Augustus W.N. Pugin to

RIGHT The Corner Drawing Room, with state portraits.

assist with the project and its detail. The collaboration – not always harmonious – was inspired and the result was a triumph. The new Houses of Parliament not only became a convincing symbol of London but also appealed to a deep atavistic feeling about the nature of Parliament, with a building that is at the same time venerable, romantic and authoritative. Countless books and films have recognized its picturesque qualities (not to mention the resonances that are provided by the sound of Big Ben).

Such was the prestige of the Speaker's office that Barry created a Speaker's House with rooms 'being designed for state purposes'. It was one of the last parts of the building to be completed and by far the grandest of nine apartments created for the officers of Parliament. Speaker Denison, elected in 1857, was the first Speaker to occupy the new house. Pugin had died five years earlier and the furnishing of the sumptuous interiors was entrusted to John Braund, 'an artist in design' who worked in Pugin's style. Holland and Sons won the tender to make the matching furniture.

Denison moved in, with his family, in January 1859 and his was the greatest influence on the final arrangement of the house, most of which he would recognize today.

Speaker Denison's hand is evident at the entrance to the house. Approached through a collegiate court, the elaborate entrance porch was put there at his insistence and above it sits his coat of arms. Heraldry and ornament, profuse in the House of Lords but rare in the Commons, were two of the components with which the significance of the Speaker was to be emphasized. This romanticism pervades the entrance and staircase. Stained glass, red carpets, Gothic lamps and Minton tiles are part of the armoury of ornament that create the *coup d'œil* looking up the stairs to the grand fireplace bearing – perhaps surprisingly – the royal arms over the symbol of Parliament, the portcullis. By the mid-nineteenth century the roles of monarch and Parliament could be celebrated as a symbiotic relationship. A portrait of Speaker Lenthall and his family on the stairs reminds us that matters were not always so harmonious.

FAR LEFT The looming presence of Big Ben.
LEFT Speaker Denison's arms vie with the royal arms.

ABOVE The dramatic staircase, leading the eye to the armorial fireplace.

A fan-vaulted cloister leads to the Speaker's study, a double-aspect room overlooking the Thames, with a stencilled ceiling and yellow Pugin wallpaper. The room is dominated by a William Kent style table from the old palace, and garnished with pleasing Pugin lamps and a Gothic letter-rack. A cabinet displays silver plate supplied by Garrards in 1835/6, engraved with royal insignia.

The Crimson Drawing Room takes its name from the silk damask walls. It serves as the Speaker's welcoming room. The room is decorated with portraits and armorial shields of previous Speakers, Braund's furniture, and some chairs from Pugin's own house at Ramsgate acquired in 1985. The

Speaker's House was extensively restored between 1979 and 1987, during the speakerships of George Thomas and Bernard Weatherill. This involved finding suitable paintings and furniture as well as replacing wall hangings, carpets and curtains in a historically correct manner. Sir Robert Cooke, MP, was an important figure in this restoration.

The Corner Drawing Room brings the collections of portraits up to date with Speakers Weatherill, Betty Boothroyd – the first woman to hold the office – and Michael Martin, the last two painted by Andrew Festing. The room has a typical Speaker's House fireplace in Purbeck marble with brass decorations. By far the grandest room, however,

LEFT The cloister.
RIGHT The Speaker's study.

is the State Dining Room, created around twelve full-length portraits of former Speakers, set in intricate panelling. This is for state banquets and the scale and decoration were planned accordingly: a massive polychromatic fireplace, beautifully detailed double doors surmounted with the royal arms and a matching ceiling. The portraits include Speaker Whitley by Glyn Philpott, with the artist's House of Commons mural in the background, commissioned by Whitley in the 1920s.

The greatest surprise of the house is the State Bedroom, bowdlerized from the former apartment of the Sergeant-at-Arms. A state bed was originally installed in Speaker's House in case the monarch wished to stay the night, particularly before the coronation. It is a reminder that Westminster is a royal palace, although no monarch has used the facility since George IV. The original bedroom, in a different part of the building, was dismantled and the bed sold off in the early part of the twentieth century. During the 1980s restoration expert Clive Wainwright of the Victoria & Albert Museum found the bed in a Welsh farmhouse; it was returned to the Speaker's House in 1986, when this room was especially created for it.

The present Speaker, John Bercow, uses the state rooms for entertaining and parliamentary official occasions. He and his young family live in a private flat on the floors above, as all Speakers have done since the days of World War II, when Speaker Clifton-Brown felt that the state rooms were no longer appropriate. Today every distinguished visitor to the Houses of Parliament is likely to be entertained in the Speaker's House. Nelson Mandela had drinks in the house, and Prince Charles and Lady Diana Spencer celebrated their engagement over dinner there.

4 CHEYNE WALK

CHELSEA

Everybody has their own Chelsea. For some it is the King's Road, for others the sturdy entrance hall to the district, Sloane Square, but the old heartland of this *quartier* is the area between the King's Road and Cheyne Walk, what Cyril Connolly called 'that leafy, tranquil, cultivated *spielraum* of Chelsea'.[1] Despite thunderous traffic noise from the nearby Embankment, nowhere has retained its charm better than Cheyne Walk, a street of superlative early eighteenth-century houses with romantic, literary and artistic associations. No. 4 is one of the best preserved, and it was home to several distinguished residents who reflect the character and history of the district.

Chelsea came into being in the sixteenth century as a 'Village of Palaces', of which the most famous belonged to Sir Thomas More. The seventeenth century saw royal interest, with Nell Gwyn and the Royal Hospital. Between 1660 and 1712 the Cheyne family, Lords of the Manor of Chelsea, gave their name to the early street development. No. 4 Cheyne Walk was built in 1718 (according to the rainwater head), when Chelsea was still sylvan and Swift wrote of its 'flowery meads'. The first resident was a William Morrison, who may have commissioned No. 4. It remains fairly unchanged, four storeys tall in two-tone bricks with flanking pilasters. The house has unusually fine wrought-iron gates, one of the most beautiful doorways in the street and, uniquely, a painted staircase. The walls show two landscapes framed by grisaille Corinthian columns and the ceiling, *Juno and the Peacock*, painted *circa* 1730 in the manner of Sir James Thornhill.

The eighteenth century saw residents of No. 4 come and go, seldom staying as long as a decade. The pleasure gardens of Ranelagh were created nearby. It was in the nineteenth century that it began to change (though Stendhal could still describe Chelsea as 'elegiac'). With mighty Belgravia

[1] Cyril Connolly, *The Condemned Playground*, London 1945, p. 194.

LEFT The perfect 'Queen Anne' ensemble.

next door, Chelsea was populated by artists and writers and became the haunt of Victorian Bohemia. When Carlyle was living in Cheyne Row (he moved there in 1834), he found Chelsea singular, dirty and beautiful all at once. In keeping with the times, 4 Cheyne Walk was a home to artists. The Scots painter William Dyce moved in when he was painting the Chamber of the House of Lords in 1846. He shared the house with the Irish artist Daniel Maclise, who was also working at the new Palace of Westminster (in the Royal Gallery). Maclise took over the lease in 1861 and lived there until his death a decade later.

Maclise's neighbour at 16 Cheyne Walk was the painter Dante Gabriel Rossetti, who remains the presiding spirit of the street. It was said that respectable artists went to Kensington and avant-garde artists went to Chelsea. Rossetti moved in – with, among others, the poet Swinburne – in 1862. They kept peacocks that were so noisy the Cadogan Estates put a special clause into their leases to ban them in future. By the end of the nineteenth century the area had a whiff of scandal about it. No. 4 was not immune, but its story was more tragic than scandalous.

Mary Anne Evans, aka George Eliot, lived 'in sin' with George Henry Lewes until his death in 1878. In her bereavement, she turned for consolation to the banker John Walter Cross, who was more than twenty years her junior.

To the disapproval of friends and fans, they married in 1880, and in the same year they acquired 4 Cheyne Walk. They went on honeymoon to Venice where – possibly in a deep depression – he fell or jumped into a canal, causing even more comment. By December they had moved into their house in Chelsea, but within three weeks she was dead from kidney disease. She was buried in a Dissenter's grave at Highgate Cemetery.

It was the trial of Oscar Wilde – who lived around the corner in Tite Street – that sealed the raffish reputation of Chelsea. Despite the presence of Henry James to raise the tone, it became an area of affordable bohemia. In the twentieth century 4 Cheyne Walk was broken up into bedsits. It was Ernest Meinertzhagen who returned the house to single occupation. The present owner has restored and maintained the house beautifully.

ABOVE LEFT Rossetti, the presiding spirit of the street, declaiming to Henry Treffry Dunn in his sitting room at No. 16: a watercolour by Theodore Watts-Dunton, 1882.
ABOVE RIGHT The exterior of No. 16.
RIGHT The painted staircase at No. 4.

LEIGHTON HOUSE

HOLLAND PARK ROAD

To visit Lord Leighton's house is to step into the world of a successful Victorian artist. His house is an anthology of his interests, from the Hellenistic and Byzantine, through the Ottoman and Renaissance, up until Eugène Delacroix. It is also a perfect statement about who he was: a bachelor who was the leading figure of the art establishment. Leighton's house is a studio and an exotic waiting room. It contains only one bedroom, for an artist who had no family and wanted no house guests. Henry James introduced Leighton into *The Private Life* as Lord Mellifont, 'a public man with no corresponding private life'. He was dedicated to his art but, like all successful Victorian artists, he needed a platform.

In common with John Everett Millais and George Frederic Watts, Leighton chose to work in Kensington, which became the favoured *quartier* for rich and fashionable painters. Val Prinsep commissioned Philip Webb in 1864 to design what was probably London's first purpose-built artist's house at

14 Holland Park Road. It was constructed in red brick and contained the obligatory blue and white porcelain of the time. The plot next door was where Leighton built his house.

Frederic Leighton (1830–1896) is the only English artist ever to be granted a peerage. He was friends with the Pre-Raphaelites, on the edge of the Aesthetic Movement and from 1878, at the age of forty-seven, President of the Royal Academy. His rise to eminence was inexorable if not smooth. He was born in Scarborough in 1830 and had a cosmopolitan upbringing. His father was a doctor who settled in Frankfurt in 1846. He spent a great deal of his early manhood travelling, picking up the influence of the Nazarenes in Germany, the old masters in Italy and the modern masters in Paris. He returned to London in 1859 one of the best-travelled artists of his generation but, following the initial success of his *Cimabue's Celebrated Madonna*, exhibited to acclaim at the Royal Academy in 1855 and bought by Queen Victoria, he

met with hostility and rejection, probably on account of the foreign influences in his work. Leighton's favoured subject matter was classical, but it was the pathos, sensuality and tension with which he imbued his paintings that gained him increasing support during the 1860s and 1870s.

It was the sale of *Dante in Exile* (1864) for 1,000 guineas that enabled Leighton to buy the plot on Holland Park Road and ask his friend George Aitchison to design a new house. Externally, it is as austere as the man himself, an asymmetrical brick building with stone banding and eccentric fenestration which anticipates Voysey. By contrast the interior is richly ornamental. The visitor is immediately plunged into the heavily layered Arab Hall. This was created to house his collection of Middle Eastern tiles and was no doubt influenced by his trips to the Near East and Damascus in 1873. The Arab Hall was a collaboration of several craftsmen, with coloured glass in the dome, Egyptian shutters, marble capitals by Edgar Boehm, a gold mosaic frieze designed by Walter Crane and tiles collected on Leighton's travels. The critic Wilfred Meynell called the Arab Hall 'a treasury of research and taste' – and it cost the artist a hefty £7,000.

The great loss to the house was the sale of the vast majority of the contents at Christie's after Leighton's death in 1896. Leighton had conceived the form and decoration of the house around these collections. Their loss compromised his original vision, but the curators have done their best to borrow appropriate paintings and objects, including a Delacroix study that once belonged to Leighton, and reinstate them in their original locations.

RIGHT Ceramic, marble, glass and mosaic – some of the many materials and techniques used in the Arab Hall.

Up the stairs, lined with peacock-blue tiles by William De Morgan and hung with Watts's thoughtful portrait of Leighton, the visitor arrives in the Silk Room, which Aitchison created in 1895 as a picture gallery. Leighton's taste in paintings centred on French and English contemporaries but included old masters such as Tintoretto and Schiavone. When he became president of the Royal Academy he extended his purchasing towards predecessors such as Reynolds and Grant. Happily, one of Leighton's contemporary paintings, Millais' *Shelling Peas*, is on loan and hanging in the Silk Room.

The exotica downstairs and the picture collection upstairs are but an overture to the studio. This is the main room in the house, to which all else is subservient, with large windows, red/brown walls, plaster casts of the Parthenon frieze and Michelangelo's *Tondo*, as well as Leighton's own paintings: *Corinna of Tangra*, *Death of Brunelleschi* and *Clytie*, the last left unfinished on his death. The oriental textiles are missing, but the landscape sketches are still there, and so is the models' access doorway from the back stairs. Much of Leighton's purchasing was bric-a-brac to act as props for his paintings and, even without this profusion, the studio remains atmospheric.

Following Leighton's death, his sisters offered the house and contents at a discounted price to create a museum. This proved impossible at the time and it emerged that, in monetary terms, the real value of the estate lay in the contents. The house, with its eccentric arrangement of rooms and its single bedroom, was unsaleable. Eventually, long after the contents had been dispersed, the house passed to Kensington Council, who have maintained it ever since and done their best to present it with pared-down contents. And in this they have succeeded, because Leighton House is first and foremost an atmosphere, not quite as strong as the Gustav Moreau Museum in Paris, but an oriental palace of someone else's dreams.

LEFT Leighton's recreated studio.

ABOVE LEFT Lord Leighton in unbuttoned mood, by George Frederic Watts, 1871.
ABOVE RIGHT Millais' *Shelling Peas*, 1891.

THE ITALIAN EMBASSY

4 GROSVENOR SQUARE

The brilliance of Mayfair was never seen to more advantage than in Grosvenor Square. It was the summit of the most glamorous district in London. Dukes, marquesses and earls rubbed alongside plutocrats whose very appearance in the square was a passport to their assimilation. Lady Bracknell in *The Importance of Being Ernest* famously imagined that the worst effects of revolution might entail 'acts of violence in Grosvenor Square'. It was secure in its position until the twentieth century, when the rush to Belgravia and an unconfident rebuild left the square not quite itself. The great houses by Robert Adam and Edward Shepherd mutated into flats for itinerant millionaires. Occupying a central position in the square, No. 4 breaks the anonymity and conformity of the apartment blocks. Above it flies the flag of Italy, which proudly proclaims this to be its embassy.

The square was created between 1725 and 1731 as the centrepiece of the Grosvenor family's Mayfair estate, and it proved to be an immediate hit. No. 4 was built about 1728 but, uncharacteristically, failed to sell until raffled a decade later. The Earl of Malton acquired it shortly afterwards and brought in Henry Flitcroft, the architect of his elongated country house, Wentworth Woodhouse. Malton's son, the 2nd Marquess of Rockingham, leader of the Whigs and twice prime minister, lived in the house, and his Fitzwilliam heirs occupied it on and off until 1931. Around 1865 the Grosvenor Estate required the house to be rebuilt. The work was done by the estate surveyor's son, Thomas Cundy III, in the Italianate style favoured by the estate at the time. When the 7th Earl Fitzwilliam surrendered the lease in 1931, the Italian Ambassador was granted a 200-year lease for £35,000 and £350 per annum.

The various states that made up Italy before unification established embassies in London during the eighteenth century. The most notable was the Sardinian, whose embassy chapel in Duke Street was known as 'the cathedral

LEFT Tapestries and busts impart a palazzo feel.

LEFT A 'subtle Italianization' – Wellesley's 1930s decoration.
RIGHT The State Dining Room.

of London Catholicism'. The kingdom of Sardinia, including Piedmont, provided the ruling dynasty of Italy from 1861 and coincidentally a majority of the subsequent ambassadors. The first embassy of the united Italy was in Grosvenor Street, but in 1890 new premises were required. The choice was between 20 Grosvenor Square and Dorchester House on Park Lane, the finest nineteenth-century palazzo in London. Legend has it that the foreign office in Rome, puzzled by Park 'Lane', looked up the word in a dictionary, to find it suggested a narrow passage, quite unsuitable for an embassy.

The Italians, having made their debut in the square at No. 20, moved to No. 4 in 1932. They employed Lord Gerald Wellesley as their architect, to transform the interior with what *The Times* called 'a subtle Italianization'. The new embassy was provided with an exceptional collection of paintings and works of art (borrowed from Italian museums), which were withdrawn after 1945. Fortunately, the first ambassador to live at No. 4, Dino Grandi (*en poste* 1932–39), left behind elements of his fine collection of paintings and furniture. Today, with a Continental mixture of tapestries, north Italian furniture and paintings, it is one of the best kitted-out embassies in London.

The entrance hall, with its marble floor, magnificent *pietre dure* table and smart uniformed *carabiniere*, announces this to be Italy. The ground-floor suite begins with the Morning Room, which contains the best paintings: Roman *vedute* by Panini, large landscapes by Alessandro Magnasco, and Luini's *Holy Family* given by Grandi. The State Dining Room, a pale yellow room, might have strayed from a north Italian palazzo. It contains the greatest treasures of the house, a set of *grotteschi* tapestries commissioned by Grand Duke Cosimo I of Tuscany in 1545 which originally hung in the Palazzo Vecchio. Their fantasy and delight disguise a serious astrological and allegorical content.

The grand marble staircase is a masterclass in restrained 1930s classicism, with its simple arches, tapestries on white walls and a bronze rococo stair rail. The first floor provides the main entertaining area. The Adam Room, overlooking the square garden, is the best room in the house, with an elaborate Cundy ceiling in the Victorian version of the Adam manner.

LEFT The Adam Room, in the Victorians' version of the architect's manner.
ABOVE The first-floor Ballroom.

It is furnished with gilt furniture and Gobelins tapestries. Next door is the former Ambassador's study, today a gallery of Savoyard portraits but also containing one surprise: a set of Lely beauties commissioned by Grand Duke Cosimo III. The room contains the only surviving chimneypiece from the Rockingham occupation of the house.

The first-floor Ballroom is a good example of Wellesley's Italianization, with a segmental tunnel vault resting on a row

of pilasters that faintly suggests Tuscany. A portrait of King Carlo Emanuele III by Clementi presides over the room; it is flanked by very fine Medici tapestries.

Realizing that an ambassador needs some cosy rooms as well as grand ones, Wellesley provided two panelled 'Venetian' rooms furnished with pretty painted furniture and rococo mirrors. The Ambassador still uses one of these for smaller lunches.

Since the sixteenth century Italy has held a special place in the affections of Englishmen. The grandeur of the embassy at 4 Grosvenor Square reflects Italy's emotional response rather than a political one. When the Grosvenor Estate rebuilt the square between 1930 and 1960 they were obliged to leave No. 4 untouched. The apartment blocks may be characterless and the hotels discreet, but the Italian Embassy remains to keep alive the convivial traditions of Grosvenor Square.

OPPOSITE The Ambassador's private dining room, with one of the Medici tapestries in the Ballroom beyond.

ABOVE A detail from the Ballroom tapestry glimpsed opposite, showing a personification of the River Arno.

LINLEY SAMBOURNE HOUSE

18 STAFFORD TERRACE

Linley Sambourne couldn't decide whether he was a gentleman first or an artist. His astonishing house is an amalgam of the Aesthetic Movement's 'House Beautiful' and a conventional aspiring middle-class home. Artistic and philistine elements sit cheerfully together, reflecting the personalities of Linley and Marion Sambourne.

Sambourne worked his way up to become the main cartoonist for *Punch*. It is difficult today to recapture the importance of that humorous and satirical magazine in Victorian life. You could write the history of the reign from the magazine alone. In addition Sambourne was an illustrator whose credits include *The Water Babies* by Charles Kingsley (1886 edition). Portly and energetic, wearing thick three-piece tweed suits at all times, there was a touch of the card about the man. He married Marion in 1874 and a year later they paid £2,000 for an eighty-nine-year lease on 18 Stafford Terrace.

The decoration and furnishing of the house was a process evolving over a lifetime. The Sambournes started with William Morris wallpaper designs and woodwork painted blue-green. The contents were high-class bric-a-brac, which Sambourne assiduously collected and to some extent upgraded, so that by 1893 he ambitiously declared, 'What you see is the very best. That has been my principle throughout: not to buy anything but what was really good.' (Interestingly, when Marion visited Oscar Wilde in Tite Street she described the sparsely furnished, brightly coloured interiors as 'weird'.)

Stafford Terrace is a no-nonsense mid-nineteenth-century Kensington development and only a protruding fern tank outside No. 18 gives a hint of the profusion within. The entrance hall sets the tone, with stained glass, encaustic tiles, photographs of classical sculpture and Morris wallpaper (replaced by their granddaughter Lady Rosse in the 1960s).

RIGHT The first-floor landing, with water feature.

The dining room displays the classic blue and white china so fashionable at the time and a large sideboard, acquired in 1877, with painted decoration and tiles. Sambourne himself painted the door panels of the room. The staircase displays his *Punch* cartoons and his masterpiece, the drawing for the Diploma for the International Fisheries Exhibition of 1883. In addition there are shells, ferns and feathers, but artistic instincts give way to gentlemanly aspirations with Leech hunting scenes. Sambourne identified with his Somerset yeoman ancestors as well as with the Kensington artistic colony.

The drawing room is powerfully atmospheric. Every inch of wall and every surface is covered. The pictures are a mixed

bag, photographs of Venice, prints after old master paintings and photographs by Julia Margaret Cameron. The furniture is English and French, mostly early nineteenth century, garnished with bronzes, boule clocks and ornaments. Above the pictures is a shelf with a row of pottery plates. The whole is vastly more than the parts, and arranged with a clever eye for effect.

OPPOSITE The dining room.
ABOVE The first-floor drawing room.

OPPOSITE Roy Sambourne's bedroom.
LEFT The morning room.

The upstairs rooms are equally fascinating. Some are the result of redecorations when Morris wallpapers were replaced with expensive embossed paper in the 1880s and 1890s. The bathroom doubled up as a developing studio. Sambourne was a keen photographer and would use the medium to aid his cartoons. He developed his photographs in the marble bath which his photographer great-grandson Lord Snowdon remembers having to fill twice to make it warm enough to jump in.

It is in the bedrooms that the Sambournes' son, Roy, comes into focus. He was sent to Eton and Oxford (with considerable sacrifice on the part of his parents) and turned out to be an easy-going bachelor stockjobber who enjoyed cricket and his clubs. Roy's great merit was to leave Stafford Terrace as a monument to his parents. He makes an appearance with photographs of Oxford parties and his favourite actresses, particularly Edna May, the star of *The Belle of New York*.

If Roy was a conventional product of his class, his sister, Maud – to whom he left the house – produced interesting progeny. One of them was the designer Oliver Messel; but it

was his elder sister, Anne, who would save Stafford Terrace. She was a great beauty, one of Cecil Beaton's muses, who first married Ronald Armstrong-Jones. Lord Snowdon was one of their two children. Secondly she married the Earl of Rosse, and they came to live at Stafford Terrace on her mother's death in 1960. It is remarkable that, at a time when Victorian taste was at its lowest ebb, Roy, Maud and Anne left the house as far as possible in its original state.

Anne Rosse carefully replaced Morris wallpapers and gently modernized the house. The most notable event of the post-war era was the foundation of the Victorian Society at Stafford Terrace in 1958 with John Betjeman and others. In 1980 Lady Rosse sold the house and its contents to the Greater London Council, who opened it as a museum and monument to a then unfashionable period. It provided the setting for the aesthete Cecil's house in the film of E.M. Forster's *A Room with a View*. Dark, alluring and overcrowded, the house conforms to every conventional idea of what a Victorian house should be, with every surface covered and every wall filled. It has achieved iconic status.

TOWER HOUSE

MELBURY ROAD

The Tower House is the most singular of London houses, even including the Soane Museum. The creation of a rich, independent architect, William 'Billy' Burges, for himself, the Tower House is a recreation of a chivalric medieval world, yet full of jokes. This imaginative transmission of the past was highly personal. A nursery, a church, a castle and a theatre, the Tower House is the most colourful and wackily decorated house of the Victorian age. Some called it play-acting, a world of pet animals, heraldry, storytelling and fireplaces disguised as battlements, yet this toy medievalism is saved from whimsy by the essential seriousness and scholarship of Burges.

William Burges (1827–1881) was steeped in the medieval world. He was the son of a successful marine engineer and as a young man he travelled throughout Europe and the Middle East, soaking up the ornamental world of Islam and early Gothic architecture. 'All architects should travel,' he once said, 'but more especially the art-architect; to him it is absolutely necessary to see how various art problems have been solved in different ages.' In fact Burges did not have much time for most ages. His focus was thirteenth-century French architecture, tinctured with an appreciation for the Byzantine. Although he was to be an 'art-architect' he studied engineering and he worked with Edward Blore on the restoration of Westminster Abbey. Influenced by Pugin's brilliant polychromatic vision of the Middle Ages, Burges evolved a richly colourful style that may have been too much for his early patrons: comparatively few of his designs were actually built.

In 1864 Burges found the patron of his dreams, John, 3rd Marquess of Bute, whom we have already encountered at St John's Lodge in Regent's Park Villas. Bute was a young

LEFT William Burges's Tower House: a castle, a church, a nursery and a theatre.

romantic, intelligent and very rich. Burges rebuilt Cardiff Castle and all but created the enchanting Castell Coch for him nearby. One may see them as a dry run for the Tower House in their ornamental medievalism, which went right down to the teaspoons. (Edmund Gosse visited the architect when he lived off the Strand and described a meal served on 'beaten gold, the cream poured out of a single onyx, and the tea strictured in its descent on account of real rubies in the pot'.[1])

In the summer of 1875 Burges was able to realize his 'long day-dream' of acquiring a plot of land in Melbury Road on which to build his palace of art. This area of Kensington had become a colony of successful artists, with Frederic Leighton, Val Pinsep, Luke Fildes and G.F. Watts all within the flick of a paintbrush. But Burges despised the fashionable 'Queen Anne' style of most of his neighbours and produced instead a thirteenth-century town house of French inspiration which looks northern European on account of its red brickwork. The main features of the exterior are the conical tower enclosing the

staircase, carefully modulated fenestration and steep gables. It was the interior, however, into which Burges poured his heart. Nearly four hundred drawings survive at the RIBA that reveal his joyful obsession with every frieze and door panel.

Externally severe, inside the Tower House is an allegory, an opera and a riot of colour and fun. Every room was endowed with a different iconography and theme. The hall, entered through a bronze-covered front door, represents Time, although the multifarious references in mosaic, stained glass and painting only partially support this: a mosaic floor with *Theseus Slaying the Minotaur*, as well as paintings of Morning, Noon, Evening and Night (and more). The dining room, dedicated to Fame, is lined with impermeable Devonshire marble and a large frieze of glazed tiles depicting popular fairy tales: *Jack and the Beanstalk*, *Little Red Riding Hood*, *Blue Beard*, and so on. The astonishing ceiling panels are enamelled iron with symbols of the universe.

The fantasy continues in the two ground-floor rooms facing the garden, the library and the drawing room (now used as a music room), dedicated to Love and the Liberal

[1] Caroline Dakers, *The Holland Park Circle: Artists and Victorian Society*, London 1999, p. 175.

OPPOSITE LEFT The entrance hall.
OPPOSITE RIGHT Burges designed his own furniture. The library bookcases have doors painted, by friends of Burges, with scenes of artists and craftsmen.
ABOVE The library, with its Tower of Babel chimneypiece.

Arts respectively. These rooms are notable for their chimneypieces. The library contains one of the most fantastic ever devised: the Tower of Babel chimneypiece in the form of a battlemented castle, with Nimrod perched in a tower. The drawing room fireplace, equally extraordinary, shows figures from the medieval *Roman de la Rose*. The room is articulated with three deep marble window recesses and arches. For all of these rooms Burges designed original painted furniture that is colourful and childishly delightful.

BELOW AND RIGHT The drawing room, now furnished by the current owner, Jimmy Page, as a music room.

There is no loss of energy upstairs in the Tower House. Burges's bachelor bedroom represents the Sea, and the guest bedroom the Earth. He studded his bedroom ceiling with tiny convex mirrors to reflect candlelight which shone on a mermaid chimneypiece. Perhaps the most surprising room in a house where everything surprises is the first-floor armoury, where Burges kept his collection of armour, long since dispersed, but known from evocative photographs. There is also a nursery, another surprising choice for the childless bachelor Burges.

The Tower House was Burges's last great work and his domestic masterpiece. An army of craftsmen created the house, unfinished at his death in 1881. It would be quite wrong to think of the Tower House as an ornamental folly, it being very solidly built with walls sometimes 2 feet thick, vast foundations and ceiling beams of 'barbaric proportions'. Burges was also a considerable scholar, who understood what a medieval interior should look like. The Tower House was much admired by contemporaries, who recognized its

authenticity but also the sheer sense of fun which saved it from suffocation. Burges died in the house shortly after a visit from Oscar Wilde and J.M. Whistler.

The subsequent history of the Tower House is a paradigm of the reputation of the Gothic revival. Some of the decorations were painted over and the contents were dispersed. By the 1960s the house was empty and vandalized, until in 1969 it was acquired by the actor Richard Harris, who started a process of restoration and reacquiring objects that has continued ever since, especially under the present owner, Led Zeppelin guitarist Jimmy Page. Let the last word be with Burges's friend W.R. Lethaby, who described the Tower House as 'massive, learned, glittering, amazing'.

OPPOSITE The drawing room fireplace, with figures from the *Roman de la Rose*.
BELOW Burges's bachelor bedroom, with its watery theme.

ASTOR HOUSE

2 TEMPLE PLACE

Tudor revival mansions were not generally the style of the London rich, and Astor House is a rare survivor. From the outside it might be a guildhall or a livery company hall. Sandwiched between the Temple on one side and the headquarters of British American Tobacco on the other, 2 Temple Place makes an unexpected appearance on the Embankment. It was built in 1895 by one of the great plutocrats of the age, William Waldorf Astor, later 1st Viscount Astor, as both a home and an office. He turned to one of the most talented Victorian architects, John Loughborough Pearson, to recreate what a great merchant's house of the time of Elizabeth I might have looked like. The result was a luxurious dwelling in that sumptuous, oak-panelled, marbled, tapestried, chandeliered luxury which exported so well to Newport, Rhode Island.

William Waldorf Astor emigrated to Britain from America in 1890, declaring 'America is no place for a gentleman'.

In the opinion of American newspapers he had merely relocated to 'the land of lust and baccarat'.[1] In 1899 Astor became a British subject (and in the same year he acquired the thirteenth-century Hever Castle in Kent, where he could indulge in more Tudor fun).

It was completion of the Victoria Embankment in 1870 that created the site of Temple Place. In 1892 Astor bought the plot, then occupied by pumping engineers, and engaged Pearson. The architect was by then an old man with a string of magnificent churches behind him, including Truro Cathedral and St Augustine's, Kilburn. He created a mansion whose external features perfectly express the interior. Facing the river is a symmetrical facade with the emphasis on the first floor, where the main rooms were usually placed in great houses until the eighteenth century. The entrance is off the busy Embankment under an oriel window flanked by two

[1] J. Mordaunt Crook, *The Rise of the Nouveaux Riches*, London 1999, p. 155.

bronze lamps by W.S Frith, which show little boys playing with the new-fangled telephone and electricity. Sharp-eyed visitors will also notice the weather vane in the shape of one of the ships with which Columbus sailed to America.

The staircase hall prepares you for the rich diet of panelling and marble. All is sumptuous, the floor of jasper, porphyry and onyx and the chimneypiece of pavonazzetto marble. The figures on the staircase from *The Three Musketeers* introduce us to one of the most unexpected features of the building, Astor's slightly burdensome literary pantheon, which unfolds throughout the house. The staircase rises to a gallery resting on ten pillars of ebony surmounted by

OPPOSITE AND ABOVE Astor's personal iconography and rich materials,
introduced in the staircase hall and the gallery, characterize the house.

characters from the work of American novelists – Fenimore Cooper, Nathaniel Hawthorne and Washington Irving – carved by Thomas Nicholls.

The Great Hall is the *pièce de résistance*. It takes up the whole of the river facade on the first floor, measuring 71 feet long by 28 feet wide and 35 feet high. It is a glorious space, a Tudor hall with Renaissance pilasters and doors. This is where Astor lived and worked. The panelling contains a frieze of fifty-four of Astor's favourite characters from history and fiction, carved by Nathaniel Hitch. They are an astonishingly varied group, ranging from Anne Boleyn to Bismarck. One can only imagine the *ennui* of visitors patiently listening to the exposition of who they all were and why they were there. Above them are figures from the Robin Hood legends: Astor found it necessary to have these gilded in order to see them properly. At each end of the room are stained-glass windows showing Swiss landscapes at sunrise and sunset by Clayton and Bell. The Great Hall leads to Lord Astor's Library, another richly panelled room, with a vast white marble chimneypiece by Frith, on which he restricted the iconography to representations of the Arts and Sciences.

After Astor's death in 1919, the house became a prestigious office, first the headquarters of the Sun Life Assurance Company of Canada, who changed its name to the rather arch 'Sun of Canada House'. In 1928, the Society of Incorporated Accountants bought the freehold, stating that the location was 'an appropriate one for the legislature, the law, finance and commerce'.[2] Unfortunately, the position also put it in the front line for the attentions of German aerial bombardment in World War II. In 1944 Temple Place was hit by a flying bomb which destroyed the front door. This might have been the end of Astor House but it was patched up and in 1960 the freehold passed to Smith and Nephew, a firm whose fortune came from feminine hygiene brands. They did something very unexpected, given the times: they restored the house and built an extension in the same Tudor style and to a similar quality by Sir Percy Thomas and Son, thereby earning the attention and praise of John Betjeman. The extension has served as the administrative office to the building ever since.

The latest chapter in this story began in 1999 when banker Richard Hoare who, correctly prophesying a stock market crash, had liquefied his shares, fortuitously heard about the availability of Temple Place. He quixotically bought the

building and established his charitable Bulldog Trust there. They have bought the house back to its former glory and made it available for a wide variety of functions.

[2] *Incorporated Accountants' Hall, its History and Architecture*, London 1953, pp. 5–6.

ABOVE George Frampton's silver-gilt panels with Arthurian characters.
RIGHT The Great Hall with its hammer-beam roof.

THE BRAZILIAN EMBASSY

54 MOUNT STREET

54 Mount Street, which since 1940 has been the home of the Brazilian Embassy, is a fine example of a Mayfair mansion built in the swansong of late Victorian confidence. It was created for a discerning and artistic patron, Lord Windsor, to the highest standards and using the richest materials. With only three occupiers since the 1890s, the fabric is remarkably untouched – as is exemplified by the unusual surviving service area in the basement.

The builder of the house, Robert Windsor-Clive (1857–1923), 14th Baron Windsor and from 1905 1st Earl of Plymouth, was an artist, patron and sportsman whose fortune derived from accumulated inherited estates of nearly forty thousand acres, of which the richest parts were the mineral mines of Glamorganshire and the outskirts of Cardiff. He is an interesting representative of an old family with new wealth. He was a friend of Joseph Conrad and a minor politician who became Paymaster General in Lord Salisbury's

administration. He was a member of the Architectural Vigilance Society, which attempted to maintain standards in London architecture.

Architecture was Lord Windsor's passion, and he almost impoverished his family as a result. His most quixotic act was to underwrite the future of the Crystal Palace, an obligation that cost him a fortune but saved the structure until it burnt down in 1936. In his capacity as First Commissioner of Works, Lord Windsor is given much of the credit for the appointment of Norman Shaw to rebuild Nash's Regent Street Quadrant. He was chief subscriber to his memorial plaque. So why did Windsor choose such an obscure figure as Fairfax B. Wade to build his London mansion?

Wade, whom we have already encountered at 3 Grafton Street (see page 82), had a small *œuvre* but was favoured by the 1st Duke of Westminster, who may have recommended him to Lord Windsor. The Duke had a vested interest, as

RIGHT The marble-lined staircase to the main reception rooms.

not only was the house on his freehold but it also overlooked his garden at Grosvenor House. What Wade created was a massive structure in the English baroque 'Wrenaissance' style, with touches of Arts and Crafts and French classicism. Externally the house is in red brick, with Portland stone dressings and a monumental projecting entrance. It was begun in 1895 and was still unfinished in 1900 when members of the Architectural Association were given a tour by Wade. 'Lord Windsor', they reported, 'possesses the somewhat rare virtue in a client, not requiring the over-speedy exit of the British workman from his domain, and he wisely prefers maturing ideas at leisure instead of hurriedly committing

them indelibly to the precious woods and marbles.'[1]

In 1919 Lord Plymouth, as he was by then, sold the lease to Weetman Pearson, later 2nd Viscount Cowdray, who brought in Sir Aston Webb's firm to make alterations to the kitchens, bathrooms and Dining Room. Lord Cowdray died at the house in 1933. Seven years later the Brazilian Embassy rented the house from his heirs, initially on an annual tenancy. They have been there ever since. Their arrival accounts for the unusual preservation of 54 Mount Street as a grand Mayfair residence.

[1] *Survey of London*: vol. 40, *The Grosvenor Estate in Mayfair*, Part II (The Buildings), London 1980, p. 325.

The entrance hall is coated in pale pink marble from Lord Windsor's Welsh quarries, with a black and white marble floor and a white vaulted ceiling. The ground-floor rooms are panelled in precious woods, the study in walnut, the Morning Room in cedar, while the Dining Room was altered by Lord Cowdray, who installed neo-Elizabethan panelling and an oak fireplace that jar with the rest of the house. The staircase and upper hall reveal Wade at his best, with a gorgeous marble confection of balustrades and a row of double Corinthian columns under an oval lantern. The back wall originally held Burne-Jones's cartoon of the *Apocalypse*, which Lord Cowdray replaced with the present tapestry.

ABOVE AND OPPOSITE Lord Windsor was notably fond of rich materials – and had the wealth to indulge his taste.

This sumptuous space leads to the main entertaining area, the Drawing Room. An essay in the English neo-baroque, it is a white-panelled room with deep plasterwork in the Wren manner that serves as a backdrop for the Ambassador's receptions.

Important and grand as the main rooms are at 54 Mount Street, the most singular parts of the house are arguably the other floors and the back parts. Lord Cowdray's ancient lift takes the visitor up to the second and third floors, which

LEFT The Ambassador's main Drawing Room, in the Wren style.
ABOVE Aldo, the footman, with the embassy dog, Ben.

ABOVE AND OPPOSITE The service area, a rare survival in Mayfair.

have early examples of the fitted cupboard, curiously placed outside the bedrooms so as not to disturb their inhabitants. The Ambassador's bathroom, put in by Cowdray, reveals a pioneering use of mirrors and chrome.

If upstairs is interesting, downstairs is a treasure trove of surviving service arrangements. The enormous basement, which is bedecked in Dutch tiles, has the old servant bell panels and a colossal Edwardian safe. In the pantry Lord Cowdray inserted an iron spiral staircase beside the dumb waiter for staff to dash up to meet the food. The 'area' is still retained, a favourite spot for the embassy dog, Ben.

One of the Brazilian diplomats, Edmundo Barbosa da Silva, offered a wartime vignette: 'The air attack on that part of London commenced on the 7th of September 1940. At the end of the reception given by the Ambassador Moniz de Aragão in the new Embassy at 54 Mount Street, a few of us went up to the terrace on the top floor of the building, which then housed the Chancery, from where we could see the Stukas doing their sinister dives.'[2] Mercifully, the embassy was left unscathed; but the war was critical to its future in another way.

The British government had accumulated a considerable war debt to Brazil in purchasing food and other necessities. Part of the proceeds of this debt were used for the acquisition of a long lease of 54 Mount Street and some of the contents. Four years later the Brazilian Embassy made another judicious purchase of a long lease on 32 Green Street, Mayfair, for use as a chancery. This had been the London home of the 4th Lord Ribblesdale (another aristocrat with new wealth) and was built between 1897 and 1899 by Sidney R.J. Smith, the architect of Tate Britain, in a similar style to Mount Street. The Brazilians are fortunate in having two first-class Mayfair houses in which to conduct their diplomacy.

[2] Rubens Antonia Barbosa, *The Brazilian Embassy in London*, London 1995, p. 42.

DEBENHAM HOUSE

8 ADDISON ROAD

'I want a palace and I want you to build it for me,' Ernest Debenham is reported to have instructed Halsey Ricardo. The result was one of the last great architectural expressions of the Arts and Crafts movement, an astonishing and original building in which Ricardo confidently brings together several styles: the Florentine Renaissance, the neo-baroque, the Queen Anne revival and the Byzantine. What separates the house from all other Edwardian artistic houses is the external use of colour and tiles, the brilliant facing of creamy faïence setting off vivid turquoise-glazed bricks and green roof tiles. Debenham House is the product of several designers who shared Ricardo's vision; they were fortunate to find a rich patron willing to put his ideas into practice.

Ernest Debenham (1865–1952), later 1st Baronet, was grandson of the founder of the Wigmore Street store Debenham and Freebody, and a successful chairman of the family firm. Ricardo, who had independent means, rarely accepted commissions but Ernest and Cecily Debenham were an exception. They were a cultivated pair who collected early Islamic ceramics, and Cecily, in particular, was a great traveller. In 1905, the year before the building of the house commenced, she visited Venice, Padua and, significantly, Ravenna. For a time the Debenhams rented a house in Melbury Road by Ricardo. They became close friends and the invitation to build a new house in the neighbouring Addison Road followed.

Halsey Ricardo (1854–1928), from a family of Portuguese Jewish origins, was the son of a successful banker and the grandson of the economist David Ricardo. The product of Rugby School, where he surely admired Butterfield's polychromatic brickwork, Ricardo was trained in the office of the Queen Anne revivalist Basil Champneys. Ricardo's son said that his father was 'an architect by profession but an artist by inclination'. Ricardo was inspired by the Arts and

LEFT The garden passage, with De Morgan tiles.

Crafts Movement and became Master of the Art Workers Guild. During the building of Debenham House, Ricardo published his 'Essay in Colour' (1909) in the *Architectural Review*. This manifesto set out his dual concerns: his ambition to create buildings using materials that would be immune to the effects of city pollution and his passionate advocacy of colour in architecture. He was sure that tiles were the answer to both points and as early as 1902 had written, 'Why should we fear to clothe whole streets in London with coloured tiles?' Ricardo persuaded Debenham to be his torchbearer.

Fortunately this was a great period for tile manufacture, and Ricardo had been in partnership with the greatest designer of them all, William De Morgan. Their business was dissolved in 1904 but some of the residue stock, including some tiles intended for Tsar Alexander II's yacht, was used at Debenham House. De Morgan also made tiles for Leighton House, but the crucial difference at Addison Road was the intention to make the outside of the building as colourful as the inside.

Debenham House was built between 1906 and 1907. The plan is a large square. The external facades are articulated with every weapon in Ricardo's armoury: Brunelleschi arches, recessed attic storey, deep cornices and unusually tall oblong chimneys. The main facings are in creamy faïence wall tiles made by Doulton and known – from their resemblance to white marble – as Carrara Ware. This complex mixture works magnificently because Ricardo knew his materials so well and could use them with confidence.

The garden passage that leads to the main entrance is covered in De Morgan tiles of flowers and peacocks. The main wonder of the house is the domed hall, a rich Byzantine feast in which Constantinople, Ravenna and Kensington Arts and Crafts meet in happy unison. The inspiration for this stately pleasure dome may have been Ernest Debenham's. In 1912 Debenham commissioned Gaetano Meo to make additional, mostly floral, mosaic decorations in the dome, while the walls were given signs of the zodiac, peacocks and portraits of the Debenham children. (Interestingly,

RIGHT The domed hall, created in 1906.

Debenham's daughter recalled that Ricardo did not want any mosaics.[1]) The tesserae were supplied by Salviati of Venice. The effect is magnificent and has a Pre-Raphaelite warmth. Mosaic rooms are extremely rare in English homes – let alone in London – and it is difficult to think of any as ambitious or powerful as the hall at Debenham House. In addition to mosaics, several kinds of marble are employed, especially around the San Vitale-like balcony openings designed by Philip Webb's protégé George Jack.

The remaining rooms inevitably have difficulty living up to the promise of the hall. The finest of them is the library, a jewel box created with five different kinds of wood, ivory and mother-of-pearl inlay. Ernest Gimson designed several ceilings in the house, in the library and also in the drawing room and the dining room.

What unites the house, whether it be the chimneypieces, the passages or the bathrooms, is the use of the brilliantly designed colourful De Morgan tiles of flowers and animals, especially fish and birds. Debenham House is the high point of this art in Britain and De Morgan's masterpiece. Halsey Ricardo described how 'this humour, so kindly, so sympathetic, laughs out in his designs: the way he treats his birds, beast, and fishes, to obey his spacing and place themselves in almost impossible situations without protest and with the suspicion of a grin.'[2]

[1] Information given to the author by Susannah Chancellor, a granddaughter of Ernest Debenham. She also commented that 'My grandmother wasn't really behind the whole thing, as she said there wasn't much room for a woman's touch!'

[2] Quoted: Stephen Calloway and Lynn Federle Orr (editors), *The Cult of Beauty: The Aesthetic Movement 1860–1890*, London 2011, p. 151.

LEFT AND ABOVE Ravenna in Kensington: the mosaics by Gaetano Meo, added 1912–13, against the architect's wishes.

Sir Ernest Debenham lived at the house until World War II. The house was sold on his death in 1952 and, perhaps inevitably, it became institutionalized. From 1955 it was home to the London College of Dance and Drama, followed by the office of the Richmond Fellowship. It was used as the backdrop of Joseph Losey's 1968 film *Secret Ceremony*, which starred Elizabeth Taylor, Robert Mitchum and Mia Farrow. In 2001 Debenham House was acquired by Mr and Mrs Robert Wallace, who returned it to domesticity and began an extensive programme of restoration. Recently the house has changed hands again and at the time of writing it was undergoing a further major restoration. When it is complete, the house will be renamed Sultan's House.

Debenham House remains a one-off. The 1914 war destroyed the desire to build such houses in London and the glazed tiles never caught on. The writer Norman Douglas shared Ricardo's puzzlement as to why 'the cherry and ageless lustre of coloured tiles should remain the monopoly of Underground stations?' Looking at Debenham House one might agree. It was William De Morgan's sister-in-law who summed up the house as 'an Arabian Night's palace of delights'.[3]

[3] Quoted: Madge Garland, 'No. 8 Addison Road, Kensington', *Country Life*, 20 November 1975, p. 1391.

BELOW Five different woods are used in the library, along with ivory and mother-of-pearl.
RIGHT De Morgan's tiles often included humorous depictions of animals.

46 GROSVENOR STREET

MAYFAIR

At the heart of Mayfair, a stone's throw from Grosvenor Square, lies the Franco-Florentine palazzo of Sir Edgar Speyer (1862–1932). Built on the grandest scale for a terraced house, 46 Grosvenor Street exudes Edwardian wealth and confidence, and yet it probably had the shortest heyday of any house in this book. It was completed in its present form around 1911. The coming of war three years later was a catastrophe for Speyer – who was charged with having German sympathies – and a decade later the house was on the market. It was never a private house again.

The 56-foot frontage of No. 46 originally held three houses. The Palladian architect William Benson occupied one of them. The houses were two by 1820–21 and the site of one of them, No. 46, was acquired by Sir Edgar Speyer in 1899. It is difficult to come to a conclusion about Speyer: whether he was a traduced philanthropist or an arrogant

tycoon who thought the rules did not apply to him. He was born in New York, the second son of a German Jewish family from Frankfurt, and followed his father in becoming a financier. His immensely successful company, Speyer Brothers, financed much of London's Underground.

Speyer married an American violinist, Leonora von Stosch, and became a British subject in 1892. He was undoubtedly a great philanthropist, contributing to the foundation of Whitechapel Art Gallery and Captain Scott's last Antarctic expedition (and he was the recipient of one of his last unposted letters), but above all Speyer was a great patron of music. He befriended Elgar, Grieg, Debussy, Grainger – and Richard Strauss dedicated *Salome* to him. He was a pillar of London's musical life.

Initially Speyer asked Arthur Blomfield the younger to make alterations to No. 46, but in 1909 he was able to

RIGHT The Gothic staircase: a pendant boss grins behind the classical facade.

acquire No. 44 and knock the two houses together. This time he went to Detmar Blow, a brilliant architect every bit as ambiguous as Speyer himself, and whose life has certain parallels. As a young man Blow was a disciple of John Ruskin and joined the Art Workers' Guild. It is difficult sometimes to reconcile the young Arts and Craft adherent with the plutocratic architect/estate manager he later became. In 1905 Blow went into partnership with the French architect Fernand Billery and together they ran a fashionable practice, often working in the Beaux-Arts tradition. Speyer turned to them to remodel his house in a manner and scale that would be equally at home on New York's Fifth Avenue.

Externally, faced in Portland stone with a heavy Florentine rusticated ground floor, No. 46 stands out from its neighbours as an entity. Internally it was never so cohesive. This was partly the result of the Grosvenor Estate's insistence on retaining two main staircases so that the houses could one day revert to being a pair, and partly owing to the melange of styles chosen by the architects.

Today the staircase in daily use is the dark oak Bruges-Gothic confection, which may be by Blomfield. The richly panelled entrance hall has been accurately described as 'a tenebrous space'[1] and on the other side, bizarrely, is the staircase designed by Billery after the Scala dei Giganti of the Doge's Palace in Venice. The opulent eclecticism continues upstairs. Facing the street is the Italian Room in a Florentine Renaissance manner, with a carved stone fireplace and heavy doors, one carved with figures from Italian history and

---

[1] Nikolaus Pevsner, Simon Bradley and John Schofield, *London 6: Westminster*, London 2003, p. 532.

LEFT The improbable Gothic staircase.

ABOVE The eclecticism continues with a Florentine room.

another with papal arms. The greatest surprise of the house – and no doubt Speyer's pride and joy – is the Music Room, a breathtaking space taking up the whole of the back of the first floor. Rarely has the Louis XV revival style been used in London to such effect. Rich orange-brown stained oak panelling is picked out with gilt pilasters and carvings under a sugary painted ceiling by Maurice Tastemain. At one end of the room there is an organ case, alas without its organ. Today the room is used as a boardroom. The second floor has former bedrooms, richly panelled mostly in the Louis XVI style and one in a Kentian English manner.

Speyer's life at his grand new home was not to be peaceful. With the coming of war he was accused of disloyalty, and even treachery, to his adopted country. Much of this may have been paranoia. Speyer attempted to resign as a Privy Counsellor and to give up his baronetcy. The Prime Minister, Asquith, supported him: 'I have known you long, and well enough to estimate at their true value these baseless and malignant imputations to your loyalty.' A post-war investigation, however, came to a different conclusion and produced evidence of activities that were unambiguously pro-German.

Despite Asquith's assurance, Speyer left England for America in 1915. He lived his last years in New York. 46 Grosvenor Street was put up for sale in 1922 and the following year sold to the American Women's Club.

Detmar Blow suffered a similar reversal of fortune. In 1916 he was appointed by the Duke of Westminster to manage the Grosvenor Estate. This was to the detriment of his architectural practice and by 1933 the Duke was having him investigated for defrauding the estate. While nothing was conclusively proved, Blow retired a broken man and died six years later.

The subsequent history of No. 46 was more cheerful. It became the Japanese Embassy until the present owners, the stockbroking firm Killik & Co., acquired it in 2000. As for Sir Edgar Speyer, he lives on in literature. He and his wife were the models for Sir Hermann and Lady Aline Gurtner in E.F. Benson's novel *Robin Linnet* (1919); and, intriguingly, Joe Mordaunt Crook has suggested that Speyer was surely the sinister villain in John Buchan's *Thirty-Nine Steps*.[2]

[2] J. Mordaunt Crook, *The Rise of the Nouveaux Riches*, London 1999, p. 155.

LEFT AND FAR LEFT The *pièce de résistance*: Speyer's Music Room.

6–9 CARLTON HOUSE TERRACE

ST JAMES'S

Today the four houses of 6–9 Carlton House Terrace, completed in 1829, are joined as the headquarters of the Royal Society, and all is serene and learned. Their history, however, was not always so peaceful, and the present building has one of the strangest stories of all. Among other things, it contains one of the most complete surviving National Socialist interiors, designed by Albert Speer 1936–37, for the German Ambassador, Joachim von Ribbentrop.

Carlton House Terrace, London's finest Regency terrace, was created by Nash, after the demolition of the Prince Regent's Carlton House, so that the Crown Estates could recoup some of the building costs of Buckingham Palace. The houses, with their breathtaking views over the Mall, were always popular, particularly with the dukes when they started to abandon their traditional palaces in the early twentieth century. What strikes the observer is the turnover of residents in each house, the average tenure being between five and ten years.

No. 6 has a relatively quiet history but the most elaborate architectural interior. The Dukes of Leinster owned the lease from 1829 to 1889, but sublet the house. It was the Argentinian millionaire Charles Henry Sandford who altered the building dramatically. He is said to have made two fortunes, one from sheep and another from an American version of eau de cologne, called Florida water. Sandford was apparently deeply impressed by the decoration at the Vatican and between 1889 and 1890 he brought in Sir Ernest George and Peto to create an Italian Renaissance palazzo with Hispanic elements. The *cinquecento* entrance hall, in pink marble with white marble pilasters, leads to the grand staircase, which is pure Hollywood. The main reception room on the first floor is an ornate gilded space in a High Renaissance manner. Today it is used as the reading room for the Royal Society, with delicious views over St James's Park and Parliament beyond.

RIGHT Nash's Regency terrace masks a 1930s surprise inside.

BELOW AND OPPOSITE Renaissance architecture at No. 6, for
Charles Henry Sandford.

No. 7 has the busiest history, with a bewildering number of residents. They included the 12th Earl of Pembroke, and the 3rd Earl Somers, who commissioned the most fashionable artist of the time, George Frederic Watts, to paint nine frescoes for the house. Today they are at Eastnor Castle in Herefordshire. By far the most colourful resident was the American Gladys, Duchess of Marlborough (1881–1977). She and her husband, 'Sunny', the 9th Duke, moved into Carlton House Terrace in 1922. The following February they held a celebrated Leap Year Ball: Winston Churchill came in a toga, Lord Birkenhead in cardinal's robes, while the Prince of Wales dressed as a clown. Gladys had a taste for literary and artistic company not shared by her ardent Roman Catholic convert husband. She hung a Cézanne in the house which her husband assured Arnold Bennett was a Van Gogh. Evelyn Waugh was invited to dinner on 30 June 1930: 'sat next to Edith Sitwell. The dining-room was full of ghastly frescoes by G.F. Watts . . . there were two ambassadors and about forty hard-faced middle-aged peers and peeresses . . . The Duke wearing the Garter – also a vast silk turban over a bandaged eye from which his little hook nose protruded.'[1]

As the Marlborough marriage deteriorated, Gladys stayed more at Blenheim and the Duke tried to prevent her using Carlton House Terrace. She had valuable possessions there, however, and in July 1933 she began a vigil and refused to move from the house, despite the presence of three rough men in the basement hired by her husband to intimidate her. The utilities were turned off and she lived by candlelight on food smuggled in by her friends. Finally, on 8 August, she moved into the Carlton Hotel. A year later the Duke held his last dinner party in the house; he died shortly afterwards. From then on No. 7 became part of the German Embassy, which had already subsumed No. 8 in 1923.

The most tumultuous history, however, belongs to No. 9, which became the home of the Prussian Legation from 1849 to 1870 and, after unification, the German Embassy from 1870 until 1939. The most tragic ambassador was Prince Lichnowsky (*en poste* London 1912–14), who strove in vain for Anglo-German peace. He gave grand dinners and the next morning would be seen walking in the park with his children and his dogs, which endeared him to Londoners. When war was inevitable, the British government despatched the wrong declaration of war down to the embassy. It was the job of Harold Nicolson, as the young duty clerk, to go down to the embassy at five minutes past eleven (midnight in Berlin) on

4 August 1914 with the correct declaration and try to swap them around. He found the Ambassador in his pyjamas in bed and noticed the original envelope unopened on his chest of drawers. Nicolson referred to a 'slight error', exchanged them and left. The Ambassador returned to Germany the following day with a guard of honour.[2]

Ribbentrop's predecessor at the embassy was Dr Leopold von Hoesch (*en poste* 1932–36), whose terrier, Giro, was buried in the garden after being caught in a lift. His tombstone is still there and reads 'Giro/Ein treuer Begleiter' (a true friend). Von Hoesch himself died *en poste* in 1936 under suspicious circumstances. There is a photograph of his coffin being taken away from Carlton House Terrace by guardsmen flanked by Wehrmacht soldiers, with the embassy staff in the background giving the Nazi salute.

Nothing, however, was to prepare the staff for the whirlwind brought upon them by Hitler's insufferable envoy Joachim von Ribbentrop, appointed the same year. He entrusted Frau von Ribbentrop with rearranging the embassy in a manner suitable to his dignity as one of Hitler's closest confidants. She went to the Führer's favourite architect, Albert Speer, who refused to come personally but oversaw the designs and appointed Piepenburg to carry out

[1] See Michael Davie (editor), *The Diaries of Evelyn Waugh*, London 1976, p. 318.

[2] Harold Nicolson, *Sir Arthur Nicolson, Bart., 1st Lord Carnock*, London 1930, pp. 425–26.

OPPOSITE Giro: the dog's gravestone.
LEFT Ambassador Ribbentrop's drawing room, c.1937.
BELOW Hitler on the Mall: the removal of Ambassador von Hoesch's body from the German Embassy in 1936.

Lord Vansittart said he had 'the sore vanity of a peacock in permanent moult'.[3] Fortunately Ribbentrop's paranoia kept him in Berlin more than London. To inaugurate their new residence, with its pastoral paintings from German museums (and her Fra Angelico), the Ribbentrops threw a party in coronation week 1937 which, with misplaced enthusiasm, one newspaper called the diplomatic party of the century.[4] By this stage a ditty was doing the rounds:

> I think we all have had a drop
> Too much of Herr von Ribbentrop
> The name by which he ought to go
> Is Herr von Ribbentrop de trop.

Ribbentrop left the embassy in 1938, unlamented. Much of Speer's work remains, particularly the staircase in cream and grey travertine marble that was said to have been a gift from Mussolini. The long enfilade of entertaining rooms facing the Mall are generally as Speer left them, the swastikas removed, and today they house the distinguished collection of portraits of the Royal Society.

With the outbreak of war the embassy was requisitioned by the Foreign Office, who gave strict instructions that nothing should be removed (in case Hitler won?); officials toiled away under portraits of Hitler.

Post-war the building held various ministries, until the arrival of the Royal Society in 1967. The Royal Society received its charter from Charles II in 1662 and had moved home several times. It occupied Arundel House at the time of its foundation and from 1857 Burlington House. Past presidents include Wren, Pepys, Newton, Sloane, Banks and Rutherford. As the oldest and most distinguished scientific society in the world, the society needed a large central headquarters for which Carlton House Terrace was perfect. They had also accumulated many historical treasures which needed housing. Lord Holford was their architect, and he made a good stab at unifying the four buildings in a simplified classical modernism that picks up where Speer left off. Nos. 6–9 Carlton House Terrace have never been in safer hands.

the project. Two hundred workmen were brought over from Munich to produce a set of spacious, dull, interiors in the stripped-down classicism favoured by National Socialism. Eighty-two telephones were installed for the private use of the Ribbentrops and the whole building was bugged. The embassy staff were relegated to the basement.

During this refurbishment – which cost 5 million Reichsmarks – Ribbentrop rented Neville Chamberlain's house in Eaton Square, which the then Chancellor of the Exchequer found 'amusing'. Ribbentrop – who became known as 'Brickendrop' – antagonized London society from the start with his Nazi salutes and gauche manner.

[3] Michael Bloch, *Ribbentrop*, London 1992, p. 100.
[4] Ibid., p. 130.

OPPOSITE AND ABOVE Albert Speer's surviving staircase and enfilade.

64 OLD CHURCH STREET

CHELSEA

London has in general been wary of modernism but a domestic masterpiece of pre-war contemporary architecture survives in the citadel of Georgian Chelsea. It is the Cohen/Hamlyn house in Old Church Street, whose sleek lines and horizontal emphasis in a vertical townscape reveal the work of two brilliant architects, Erich Mendelsohn and Serge Chermayeff. They worked together briefly in England in the 1930s, producing only three buildings in partnership, each perfect within its limitations. The Cohen house was the last and the only one in London. It is still lived in today by the second family to occupy the house.

The patron behind No. 64 was Denis Cohen, a publisher who owned the Cresset Press, the aim of which was to bring high-quality books to all. He was also a director of PLAN Ltd, a company that sold well-designed modern interior furnishings for which Chermayeff designed chairs. Cohen was related by marriage to the playwright Ben Levy, whose wife was the actress Constance Cummings. Together the Cohens and Levys bought adjacent plots on Old Church Street, with the intention of building complementary modernist houses. Although primarily Georgian, the area already possessed twentieth-century houses by Halsey Ricardo and Oliver Hill, but nothing that challenged the prevailing aesthetic in the way Nos. 64 and 66 were to do. Levy chose Walter Gropius and Maxwell Fry for their plot, but there is no doubt that Cohen got the more interesting house.

Cohen's architects were unusually fascinating. Erich Mendelsohn (1887–1953) was an intellectual who could claim friendship with Einstein, Gide and Albert Kahn. He almost became a stage designer and took to drawing visionary buildings during his time in the German army at the front in World War I. Between 1920 and 1924 he built the famous Einstein Tower in Potsdam, in its sculptural appearance often

LEFT The Hamlyns' library, once Denis Cohen's squash court.

cited as the masterpiece of Expressionist architecture. He arrived in England in 1933 as a Jewish refugee and formed the brief but effective partnership with Chermayeff.

Serge Chermayeff (1900–1996) came from a well-to-do Russian family who sent him to prep school in England followed by Harrow, where he won art prizes. The outbreak of the Russian Revolution forced him to stay in England, where he developed a passion for dancing. After a false start as editor of *Dancing World* he became director of the Modern Art Department of Waring and Gillow in 1928. There was a touch of Art Deco about his work at this period. Chermayeff, who was good-looking and sociable, became a part of the modernist establishment, a member of the Finella circle and later of the MARS group, so he was a natural for Mendelsohn to team up with in London.

The masterpiece of the partnership is the De La Warr pavilion at Bexhill-on-Sea, East Sussex (1934–35), an exciting piece of marine architecture that anticipates many of the features of Old Church Street: the geometry, the asymmetrically placed semicircular bow window, the use of polished chrome and the sweeping staircase. It was around the same time that Denis Cohen asked the two architects to design a home that would provide a setting for his important collection of oriental art and Chinese ceramics. He also wanted a squash court, a problem only resolved by tucking it at one end of the house, slightly submerged. The division of labour was broadly Mendelsohn's structure and Chermayeff's fittings, but the two are entirely harmonious.

Externally the house embraces the garden and all the main rooms overlook it. The garden front with its semicircular

ABOVE LEFT Eric Mendelsohn (third from the right) at work.
ABOVE RIGHT Serge and Barbara Chermayeff.

OPPOSITE The garden front by Mendelsohn.

window and balcony has the jaunty nautical air of Bexhill, but with rare species in the garden the note is also Asiatic. The street facade is functional, a long rectangle with L-shaped first floor. The modulated fenestration is the means of expressing changes of internal function but, as John Summerson perceptively wrote in 1937, 'The modern movement, like the Elizabethan renaissance, is essentially a romantic movement . . . however rigidly it excludes ornamentalism, its mainspring is all the time romantic and irrational.'[1]

Alan Powers, Chermayeff's biographer, pointed out that 'The construction was not as pure as it looked, consisting of brick with steel beams, holding hollow slab tiles to make the roof and main floor plate, all covered with a white render that deteriorated during the war.'[2] Chermayeff said later that it was one of the pleasures of living in a white house that had to be paid for. The flat roof was to be a problem from the

start, and the Blitz blew out all the windows. One wartime visitor was the scientist Lancelot Law White, who spent a night at the house: 'In Old Church Street we reached a door in the blackout, Cohen opened it, switched on the lights, and there was the most brilliant interior I have seen in London. It was a Mendelsohn house, marvellously clean and bright, with Chinese pottery decorating the living-room . . .'[3]

Denis Cohen died in 1969 and his widow, Mary, decided to sell the house to the newly married Paul and Helen Hamlyn. When the Hamlyns acquired No. 64 it was evident that nothing had been touched since it was built and it required a complete renovation. Pilkington's rebuilt the windows and all the chrome work needed careful restoration. The Hamlyns brought the house up to date in a subtle and sensitive manner. It was gratifying to them that when Chermayeff returned to the house years later he approved of their alterations.

Paul Hamlyn (1926–2001), like Mendelsohn, was a German émigré who arrived in London in 1933 to seek a new life. His meteoric publishing career, based like

[1] Quoted: Alan Powers, *Serge Chermayeff: Designer, Architect, Teacher*, London 2001, p. 86.
[2] Ibid., p. 87.
[3] Ibid., p. 88.

Cohen's on books for all, through the Paul Hamlyn Group and Octopus Books, was followed by an equally energetic career as a philanthropist. The British Museum and Covent Garden are only two of the institutions that have been helped enormously by the Paul Hamlyn Foundation, the gift of a man who wished young people to benefit from the opportunities England gave him.

To enter 64 Old Church Street through the bronze door is to step into a harmony of beautifully crafted, restful rooms. The Hamlyns both enjoyed Asiatic artefacts, as Denis Cohen had, and these help create the atmosphere of purity and restraint. The sitting room in a light taupe is dominated by the bow window and epitomizes the indoor/outdoor East meets West theme of the house. The absence of doors on the ground-floor garden front creates a flow from the sitting room through the study to the dining room. The last two, panelled in pale sycamore, have all their original Chermayeff fittings and furniture. They have the minutely crafted perfection of a luxury boat. The detail is everything and the dining-room ceiling lights are glass blades that anticipate Rolls Royce jet engines. The old squash court was carefully adapted by Norman Foster in 1993 into a split-level library, with a gently inclining walkway into the heart of the room looking on to the garden. Foster also redesigned the conservatory, where once Helen Hamlyn kept her aviary of parakeets, Chinese robins and zebra finches.

OPPOSITE The sitting-room bow window.
LEFT The dining room, with furniture by Chermayeff.

The chrome staircase, with its large square window on to the road, is pure Bexhill. It sweeps the visitor up to the first floor with its pioneering built-in cupboards and sycamore bedroom fittings. The bathrooms have a hint of Art Deco, with their large taps and onyx finish and early examples of the shower.

Apart from Foster's additions, the house remains a virtually untouched design by Mendelsohn and Chermayeff. In 1936 Chermayeff made a BBC television programme in which he discussed 64 Old Church Street in front of a model of the house. The architect described his attempt at 'tidying up everything and simplifying' and added that 'against that simple background the particular individual arts of architecture, and painting, and sculpture can flourish like flowers cleared of weeds.'[4] Let that be its epitaph.

[4] See television talk between John Gloag and Serge Chermayeff, Avery Archive, quoted: Powers, p. 89.

BELOW LEFT Norman Foster's conservatory.
BELOW CENTRE AND RIGHT Sleek modernism: the staircase
and a bathroom.

2 WILLOW ROAD

HAMPSTEAD

Ernö Goldfinger was the quintessential Hampstead intellectual. Hungarian by birth, Continental in outlook, he and his painter wife, Ursula, were missionaries for modernism. Hampstead in the 1930s replaced Chelsea as the quarter for avant-garde writers and artists. Herbert Read referred to his neighbours in Parkhill Road, who included Ben Nicholson, Barbara Hepworth and Henry Moore, as 'a gentle nest of artists'. Into this milieu, Goldfinger bounced like a noisy dog. No. 2 Willow Road, completed in 1939, was to be his home, his manifesto and his proving ground as an architect.

Ernö Goldfinger was a larger-than-life character, of great charm but also subject to great rages. His strong personality etched itself into the fabric of his house. Born in Budapest in 1902, the son of a wealthy lawyer, Goldfinger went to Paris in 1920 to learn French and after a false start in sculpture went to the Ecole des Beaux-Arts to study architecture. Frustrated by its conservatism, he later wrote 'At the Beaux-Arts

everything was dead. All this stirring of modern architecture was ridiculed . . . we weighed up whether we should ask Le Corbusier or Perret to teach us architecture.'[1] He chose Auguste Perret, whose theories of 'structural rationalism' and belief in the use of modern materials such as concrete within a classical framework appealed to the young architect. Helena Rubinstein brought Goldfinger to London for the first time in 1927 to design a modernist salon at 24 Grafton Street. Two years later he set up a partnership in Paris and was lucky to find jobs from progressive clients such as Lee Miller and the lawyer Suzanne Blum. Goldfinger no doubt expected that Paris would remain his home, but in 1931 he met and fell in love with Ursula Blackwell, an art student, whose family had the Crosse and Blackwell soup fortune. 2 Willow Road began as a studio-cum-house for her which rapidly developed into a house for the two of them. They

[1] Alan Powers, *2 Willow Road* (National Trust guidebook), London 1996, p.6.

LEFT The view up the Heath, from the dining room.

married in 1933. Willow Road was completed in 1939, and they brought up their three children there.

Using Ursula's money they had bought four small cottages facing Hampstead Heath. The idea was to demolish them and build a block of flats, but the proposal was rejected by the planning authority. The plan then moved to building three houses on the site; live in the central one, sell one and rent the other to recoup costs. Eventually both flanking houses were sold. Although a committed modernist, Goldfinger admired the simplicity of the Hampstead Georgian terraced houses and wanted to create a design that respected that tradition. In the event his design was controversial and attracted strong opposition from the Hampstead Protection Society, which surprised the architect. It was manifestly not a modern white box but an elegant structure using brick, metal, wood finish and concrete pillars, and featuring a horizontal window band on the first floor that stretched right across the three houses. With a few alterations, such as reducing the window area, Goldfinger eventually got his design through the planners.

Inside Willow Road light is all important. The hall is low, with opaque glass on either side of the front door framed by shelves with objets trouvés. The staircase is at the core of the house under a skylight so that the living rooms receive maximum light from the windows. The concrete stairs (covered in cork) rise with brass handrails contrasting with rope banisters. The dining room on the first floor faces the Heath. On this floor we can discern the influence of Adolf Loos with his theory of domestic arrangement called 'space plan', which 'conceived a house as a series of volumes fitted into a plain exterior envelope'[2], each distinctive in character through variations of height, level, and colour. The dining room has one wall painted Etruscan red, the other two being white, enlivened by a Roland Penrose collage and works by Max Ernst, Ozenfant (who became Ursula's teacher) and Bridget Riley. The long horizontal window is deceptive, as the lower section of glass

2 Ibid., p. 7.

is projected to provide a shelf. Much of the furniture in the house was designed by Goldfinger himself.

Adjacent to the dining room, separated by a folding partition, was Ursula's studio, which Ernö took over during the war. The most striking elements are the desk with cantilevered drawers (to make it easier to reach the back) and a tool box – which emphasizes Goldfinger's belief in the hands-on nature of architecture as a craft. A step, which is also a storage space, leads to the living room, which holds the lion's share of the art, and is faced in oak plywood. On one wall is a framed screen – a Surrealist device – on which he hung small works of art, placing books along the base. The room contains art works by Henry Moore, a photograph of Ursula by Man Ray, a kinetic Duchamp and a pebble by Max Ernst. The lighting follows designs Goldfinger made for a cinema and a small rather nautical clock is mounted in the wall. Attention to detail is everything. The study contains many of the family's art books, relics such as Auguste Perret's top hat, a copy of Ian Fleming's novel that cheekily borrowed

the architect's surname, and a separate bookcase of Michelin and Baedeker European guides.

The top floor contains the main bedroom, with a low Japanese-style bed. Ursula insisted on a carpet in this room. Clever storage spaces and fitted cupboards, a vogue of the 1930s, are a feature of Willow Road. There was always a spare bedroom. The Goldfingers entertained a great deal and many of their foreign friends came to stay. As their son, Peter, pointed out, some guests came for a week and stayed a year. The children had a nursery perfectly designed for a modernist childhood, with wooden toys: aeroplanes, trains, boats and even a modernist doll's house made by the architect himself.

ABOVE LEFT The entrance hall.
ABOVE CENTRE The spiral stairs, with light effects.
ABOVE RIGHT The dining room flows into the studio.

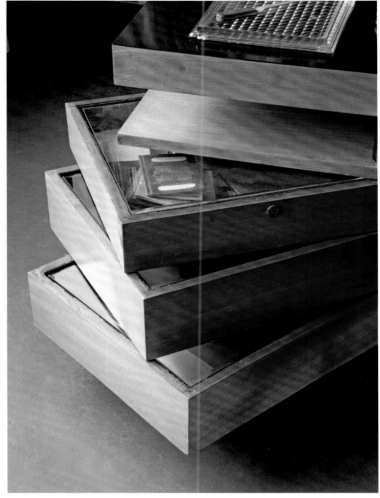

LEFT AND ABOVE Goldfinger's studio, with his desk.

When the children grew up Ernö's mother, Regine, moved into a section of the nursery and brought with her old master paintings and vast pieces of Austro-Hungarian furniture, which made a comical contrast to everything else in the house.

Ernö Goldfinger was never a prolific architect. He was on the post-war Greater London Council (GLC)[3] list of

approved architects and designed the unloved Alexander Fleming House complex at Elephant and Castle (1962–67), as well as two celebrated London high-rise residential blocks, Balfour Tower (1965) and Trellick Tower (1972). By the 1970s Goldfinger's tough aesthetic of exposed concrete was already going out of fashion. However, when he died in 1987 the house in Willow Road was recognized as a classic of its time. With the help of the family, the National Trust acquired it in 1994, its first modernist house, and it was

[3] Whose architectural office was described by Jim Richards as 'a great empire in which the concrete never sets'.

opened to the public two years later. Goldfinger was always a
passionate advocate of the modern and Willow Road makes
few compromises. As he wrote to Ursula in 1931, 'Goodness,
love, art; they are in our heart and in us, and they will not be
satisfied by little shows of propaganda.'[4]

[4] Ibid., p. 4.

ABOVE LEFT Ernö Goldfinger at Trellick Tower.
ABOVE RIGHT Goldfinger with his mother, Regine, in her room filled with Austro-Hungarian furniture.

10 MILNER STREET

CHELSEA

Milner Street is as pleasant a spot as you will find between South Kensington and Cadogan Square. No. 10 is distinctive because of its wide palazzo appearance, long windows and orange/ochre walls, which hint at the 1960s. This is not misleading, for inside is one of the most ingenious and evocative creations of a leading interior designer of the era, Michael Inchbald. Today his name is best known for the Inchbald School of Design (founded 1960) but in the post-war era he was an innovator and style-maker whose house in Milner Street was his emblem, showroom and workshop of ideas.

The house was built in 1850 in the Italianate manner that preceded the 'Pont Street Dutch' style of its Cadogan estate neighbours. Michael's grandmother acquired the freehold around 1910 because she liked its dimensions – its width being greater than its height. With the house came an old manservant who lived under the kitchen sink and wore a tail

coat several sizes too long, making him look like a beetle. She bequeathed the house to her son, Michael's uncle, Courtenay Ilbert, who was a celebrated horologist and clock collector. He was a bachelor who lived amidst the cacophony of a thousand clocks (and two thousand watches) – which Michael later sold to the British Museum for £40,000 to set himself up in business.

Michael Inchbald was an artistic but driven child who loved drawing and somehow got through Sherborne and wartime soldiering. He studied at the Architectural Association, the nursery for modernist architects, which he rebelled against. When he went to live with his uncle at Milner Street, he took the opportunity to develop one, and then two, rooms to show what he could do. He won three design prizes at the Festival of Britain. Peter Jones – then a leader of design – took him up and he also opened an antique

RIGHT Inchbald designed modern furniture and used new materials.

shop. Gradually he evolved a distinctive 'Inchbald look' of modernist lines, often with classical objects. Above all he was the product of the war, shortages and make-do-and-mend ingenuity (this stayed with him his whole life – to the end many of his letters would be written on scrap paper and sent in reused envelopes). Commonplace materials must be made to look expensive. His aesthetic was born out of a junction of modernism and a selective form of classicism.

Inchbald inherited 10 Milner Street around 1956 in a terrible state of repair. He restored it, lengthened the windows, and decorated it in two campaigns, 1956–60 and again in the 1970s as his style developed. He designed Dunhill's Jermyn Street shop but his two biggest clients were the Savoy Group of hotels and Cunard, for whom he designed the head office as well as parts of the *Queen Elizabeth II* liner. The Berkeley Hotel ballroom (no longer surviving) and the Queen's Room, the first-class lounge of the *QEII*, are often cited as his masterpieces, but his house

at Milner Street offers an array of fascinating evidence about a period whose works are fast disappearing.

The entrance hall of No. 10 sets the tone, with theatrical felt cut-out door surrounds, which are both simple and effective, and a door hinged in the middle to save space. One of his greatest skills was visually manipulating awkward spaces. Ingenious use of space and improbable storage areas, so characteristic of the 1960s, are a big feature of the house, along with mirrors to create an illusion of extra space. The dining room has a 1970s French feel, with bold floral weave wallpaper, a French chimneypiece and chairs, whereas the library evokes northern Italy: heavy bookcases, shutters, busts in recesses, columns, globes and a marble table. The library ceiling is wood veneer and the 'distemper' walls were done by a fashionable painter of decorative effects. The screen turns out to be a cupboard.

Walking upstairs is to go back a decade, into the 1960s. The stairs have distressed silvered wallpaper, blackamoors and a mirror cut in half to reveal a storage space. The sitting room

OPPOSITE The eclectic
entrance hall and tent-like
door surround.
LEFT The dining room in
1970s French style.

at first glance appears quite conventional but gradually one becomes aware of its originality. It is claimed that this was probably the first sitting room in the world to have a lino floor, and it remains in good condition. The walls were originally orange velvet and here lies a paradox. The reds and oranges so beloved of the 1960s were often used by Inchbald (despite the fact that he was colour-blind). The furnishings are mostly antique – a portrait of Louis XV, a French commode – but also include a white plastic Lurashell chair he designed for the *QEII*. Inchbald extended the back of the sitting room over the garden, with a working area featuring cork-faced cupboards and a collapsible desk. There is a gimmicky 'tomorrow's world' aspect to much of this, with echoes of Ian Fleming's novels. Nothing is what it seems.

Inchbald was no respecter of antiques. Speakers were mounted in cabinets and lights drilled through walnut furniture. His bedroom at first appears to be an extension of the sitting room, with beds disguised as sofas and cupboards (a passion for them) in concealed places. Walls are covered in basketweave and even in pegboard/perforated hardboard. The bathroom with its pastel mosaic pieces has another feature of the period, a sliding door. It is the junction of modern practicality and antique effects that defines the house. I was reminded of something that Myfanwy Piper wrote about Reynolds Stone: 'He has escaped the menace of bloodless good taste; the past is for him not a goal but a weapon.'[1] Michael Inchbald's house is a classic of its time.

[1] Myfanwy Piper, *Reynolds Stone: Engravings*, London 1977, p. 34.

OPPOSITE The sitting room with lino floor and velvet wall coverings.

BELOW Inchbald's bedroom, straight from an early James Bond film.

SPITALFIELDS HOUSES

I went down to Spitalfields to find a house and found a community. No single house could quite tell the story of this area, which is an inspiring tale of a band of architectural enthusiasts turning the tide of demolition and development. What they achieved is one of the great victories of conservation, and the area has become one of the most sought after in London.

The revival began with architectural historians, including Dan Cruikshank, in the 1970s. Then the artists came: Gilbert and George were early colonizers and a later arrival is Tracey Emin. There are two clusters of eighteenth-century streets on either side of Commercial Street and the old Spitalfields fruit and vegetable market. Looming over all is the greatest of London churches, Hawksmoor's Christ Church Spitalfields, a totemic presence which architecturally unites the community today as it did in the eighteenth century.

The history of Spitalfields has always been a community story. The area was developed around the medieval priory and hospital of St Mary Spital, which was closed in 1538. By the late seventeenth century Spitalfields, just outside the City walls, had become residential and a hotbed of nonconformity, attracting Jewish immigrants and – after the revocation of the Edict of Nantes by Louis XIV in 1685 – the Huguenot silk weavers who left the strongest imprint on the area. It was against this background of nonconformity (the first Baptist church in England was established here in 1612) that Hawksmoor's Christ Church and his other East End churches were erected, intended to serve as a counterblast.

The Huguenots built many of the handsome early eighteenth-century houses, in which they both lived and worked, and they brought prosperity to Spitalfields. But by Victorian times the silk industry was in terminal decline.

LEFT Nos. 14 and 12 Fournier Street.

Attempts were made to establish new trades. There was a wave of German immigrants, and of Ashkenazi Jews from Eastern Europe, many of whom came in hope of work as tailors. But the area was mired in poverty; and squalor and crime stalked the streets. Sweeney Todd was born next to Folgate Street and the area became the roaming ground of Jack the Ripper. The building of Commercial Street in 1864, the rebuilding of Spitalfields Market in the 1880s and the attentions of Victorian philanthropy began to alleviate the distress. The final wave of immigrants arrived from Bangladesh and Bengal in the 1970s. Nowhere is this changing character better reflected than in the mosque in Fournier Street. Built as a Huguenot chapel in 1743, in the early nineteenth century it became a reception centre for Jews converting to Christianity, then a Methodist chapel, in 1897 an orthodox synagogue and finally, in 1975, a mosque.

Poverty preserved Spitalfields until the 1960s when, as the City of London encroached, it began to attract developers. Conservationists squatted in the houses while the demolition men were outside. The Spitalfields Trust was formed in 1977 by Mark Girouard, among others, to buy properties with a revolving fund, apply first aid, and resell to enthusiasts; to whom the ownership of a Georgian house became a hobby, a way of life and an obsession. There were surprising numbers of them and a pioneering spirit was abroad. The Bengali community and Brick Lane Market were neighbours and provided an exotic backdrop. Four houses serve to demonstrate the changing face of the area.

Fournier Street is the main street of parade. It attaches itself like a tail along the back of Hawksmoor's Christ Church and was developed in its wake from 1726, largely by three builder/carpenters, Marmaduke Smith, Samuel Worrall, and William Taylor. Typical is No. 4, built by Smith for himself. It was also

his show house and has a double-width frontage, stone floors and particularly fine panelling and staircase. The first-floor bow window in the drawing room from the 1780s reveals the last flourish of Spitalfields wealth before the present time. The house declined sharply during the Victorian era, when several families were in occupation and it was also used for warehousing and cottage industries. No. 4 was sold in 1979 by the Spitalfields Trust to Michael Gillingham, art dealer, aesthete and architectural enthusiast, and Donald Finlay. Gillingham died in 1998 and the present owners, Christopher Legge and Eleanor Jones, maintain the house with care.

No. 3 Fournier Street tells a nice story of a house reverting to being an artisan workshop and dwelling. Marianna Kennedy makes contemporary furnishings here, while her bookbinder husband, Charles Gledhill, pursues his craft on the top floor, from which he has views through chimney pots on to the church.

OPPOSITE LEFT A view of Elder Street.
OPPOSITE RIGHT The staircase in Worrall House, Princelet Street.
ABOVE No. 3 Fournier Street, where Marianna Kennedy and Charles Gledhill live and work.

LEFT No. 31 Fournier Street:
a fireplace from Oscar Wilde's
house in Tite Street.
RIGHT No. 18 Folgate Street:
period rooms confected by
Dennis Severs.

Rodney Archer, a man of the theatre, acquired 31 Fournier Street in 1980 and was typical of the pioneering spirit of the time, searching for architectural salvage and appropriate contents on a shoestring. He managed to buy a fireplace from Oscar Wilde's house in Tite Street for £10. This is now the centrepiece of his sitting room.

The Spitalfields house that has always attracted the most attention is on the other side of Commercial Street, 18 Folgate Street, the home of Dennis Severs. He was an American romantic who fell in love with England and first settled in Dorset. In 1979 Severs bought the dilapidated house in Folgate Street, which had been used as bedsits for market workers, and slowly he developed it into the setting for an imaginary story of Huguenot weavers, the Jervis family. Each room is a *tableau vivant* which describes a separate chapter and period in their history. Peter Ackroyd, a friend of Severs, called him 'a romancer and novelist', but the fiction was very real to its creator. Severs invented a new art form at Folgate Street, part

Madame Tussauds, part National Trust and part theatre. When he died he left his imaginative confection to the Spitalfields Trust, who continue to open the house to the public.

I first encountered Spitalfields in 1979, when the first wave was already established but Fournier Street still had a darkened, forlorn, abandoned feel to it and the church was ingrained with three hundred years of soot. Today the scene has dramatically changed. Most houses have been restored and in the case of Folgate Street whole blocks have been recreated in a contemporary Georgian idiom. Spitalfields Market closed in 1986, which signalled the change: the area could now be considered as a safe investment. But the market buildings became the subject of an intense preservation campaign which happily succeeded, and they remain the home of stalls and small retailers. The church has been restored and the story of Spitalfields continues.

ABOVE AND RIGHT No. 18 Folgate Street, the Dennis Severs experience.

RICHARD ROGERS HOUSE

CHELSEA

On a corner of St Leonard's Terrace and Royal Avenue in Chelsea, part of a pleasant 1840s stucco row, lies a pair of joined-up houses, inconspicuous by day but tantalizingly lit up at night, that constitutes the most exciting modernist conversion in London. This is the home of Richard and Ruth Rogers, leading architect and chef respectively. As a couple they have captivated the creative elite of London and the house is a meeting place for politics, television and the arts. Lord Rogers is not only the designer of several cultural landmarks, including the Pompidou Centre in Paris and Lloyd's of London, but he has also been chairman of both the Tate Gallery and New Labour's Urban Task Force. St Leonard's Terrace represents the private face of a public man.

Sir Christopher Wren never succeeded in rearranging the city of London but there is one piece of town planning that the architect approved in 1681 that still survives, the axis from the Royal Hospital and Burton's Court through Royal Avenue, part of a proposed carriage link between Chelsea and Kensington Palace. The avenue, originally lined with chestnuts, today has lime trees, but it never got further than the King's Road. The Rogers house lies on the corner of this axis. The area is wonderfully unspoilt, with copious green space; it remains the Chelsea of aquatint.

St Leonard's Terrace was favoured by writers. Logan Pearsall Smith, the sage of Chelsea, lived next door at No. 11, Bram Stoker down the road at No. 18, and Ian Fleming placed James Bond's fictional address around the corner. And who was St Leonard? He was a Merovingian noble turned hermit who became the patron saint of prisoners.

Lord Rogers comes from an Anglo-Italian family and he was born in Florence. His father, a doctor, was an Anglophile, and Richard was brought up with a romantic idea of England. An awareness of design came from his mother,

RIGHT The stucco facade masks a sleek modernist interior.

who was a craftsman potter; he still keeps a collection of her beautiful white ceramics. Another influence was his cousin, the modernist architect Ernesto Rogers. The family came to England when Richard was a child and settled in Godalming and then Epsom. As a student he was entranced by the work of Sir John Soane and still finds his house in Lincoln's Inn an inspiration. Choosing to follow his cousin into architecture, he studied at the Architectural Association in London and at Yale (with Norman Foster), under Serge Chermayeff, the architect of 64 Old Church Street.

Returning to London on graduation, Rogers lived in Belsize Park and then Notting Hill before finally coming to rest in Chelsea. Belsize Park offered Rogers and his young family a vision of a pleasant suburb, but it was when Rogers and Ruth, his second wife, were living in Paris at the time of the building of the Pompidou Centre, his first high-profile project, that he discovered the joys of horizontal living. In Chelsea he was to turn the verticality of the terraced house into a horizontal flow.

Richard Rogers has built surprisingly few houses. There was one which he built with his first wife, Su Rogers, for her parents, near Falmouth. He describes it as a concrete box. He later built a house for his own parents in Wimbledon, inspired by Frank Lloyd Wright. The main material there was steel, which makes it a credible forerunner to the Chelsea house. Rogers told me that he was much influenced

by Californian houses, their flexibility, speed of construction and cost control; plus all the advantages of their being constructed off site. In fact, had any sites been available, he would have preferred to build from scratch in Chelsea.

Rogers bought the house from the Earl and Countess of Airlie some twenty-eight years ago. The Airlies had begun expanding laterally, acquiring the flats next door as their family grew, a process completed by Rogers. As he points out, the typical London terraced house has a natural rhythm, with its 15-foot span and its rectangular construction, which offers a surprising flexibility. The eventual design was an organic development, Rogers recollects, and the plan emerged gradually as he gutted the two houses and

BELOW LEFT Split levels converge on the living room.
BELOW CENTRE The kitchen is at the heart of the living space.
BELOW RIGHT An upper shelf contains a meeting area, desk and library.

reconstructed everything anew over the course of a year. One of the houses had war damage, which made planning permission easier to obtain. When the letter arrived from the council, it contained the tongue-in-cheek sentence 'Permission will be granted as long as there are no ducts on the outside.'

Coming up the irregular, diagonal glass-and-steel entrance hall staircase the visitor arrives in the dramatic main living space on the first floor of the building. There are five steel organ pipes at the top of the stairs which contain ducts for plumbing, heating and electricity. Eighty per cent of the building is taken up by the central living area, an exhilarating double-height space that Rogers calls the 'piazza'. Apart from enjoying a large family, which includes eleven grandchildren, Richard and Ruth Rogers meet people and entertain here. It is all about circulation. One is put in mind of a medieval hall, an open space for living, eating and enjoying life.

Richard Rogers speaks a lot about flexibility and the joys of lightweight steel. The main room boasts steel girders, a flying open steel staircase and natural light from twelve sash windows. As it is on a corner the sun pours in on both sides (he punched through four blind windows on the short wall). The artificial lighting in the living area is supplied by four stage lights, which are not only practical but also provide the dramatic nocturnal effects from the street. At the heart of the living space is the kitchen. Ruth Rogers is the renowned chef of the River Café and food, family and entertaining are at the heart of their life. The main room is decorated with a big Warhol of Mao, works on paper by Cy Twombly and Rogers's mother's pottery arranged like a series of Morandi paintings.

LEFT Few sitting rooms can boast such views, outside and in.

The essential construction points are a steel girder running up the height of the house which intersects with a horizontal steel girder that supports an open shelf, 12 feet wide, containing a meeting area, desk and library. The steel staircase rises dramatically to this floor and leads to the bedrooms. Almost everything in the house is especially designed, including the clean-lined furniture and the pale ash floors.

The view out of the windows is one of the most delectable that London can offer, looking over Burton's Court towards Christopher Wren's Royal Hospital. The scene is animated by children playing football, which delights Rogers. The back of the house contains many surprises: a discreet staircase leading to the children's bedrooms, and windows facing down Royal Avenue towards the King's Road, which gives the house views on a third axis. From the roof terrace, with its decking floor, the family can enjoy one of the best roofscapes in London.

Richard Rogers sums up the house in a no-nonsense way: 'keeping the scale of the terrace to preserve the area, but creating what suits you internally'. The building has withstood the test of time and maintains the elements of excitement and surprise. It stands in the tradition of London architects' houses, from Sir John Soane onwards, that provide a graceful setting for both public and private life. More than anything else, Richard Rogers' home reflects the brilliant use of technology to redefine a traditional urban arrangement.

OPPOSITE The architect's statements continue at the bedroom level, where, again, all is light and sharp, clean lines.
ABOVE Richard Rogers designed much of the furniture for the house, including the yellow headboard for the bed.

THE JENCKS HOUSE

HOLLAND PARK

Charles Jencks is the pope of postmodernism and his London home is his temple of ideas and experiment. He has rebuilt this Victorian terraced home as the Thematic House, a showcase of symbolic and semantic architecture. The house operates at three levels: functional, aesthetic and symbolic. You could know nothing of the elaborate and seemingly endless double meanings but still, as in William Burges's Tower House, simply enjoy the fun and quality of the visual feast.

Who can define postmodernism? In 1977 Jencks published *The Language of Post-Modern Architecture*, which opened the debate. Take multivalence, fragmentation and adhocism and mix them together to form Radical Eclecticism and you are in the right direction. Then, take the classical language of architecture, turn it upside down and brighten it up with art deco, pop art, surrealism and Biedermeier. What emerges is witty, parodic and often kitsch. The Jencks House plays down the pop art and the kitsch but in every other respect

it is the house that defines the movement. Jencks sees his house as a polemic against Robert Venturi's confusion over the difference between a sign and a symbol; and a critique of modernist functionalism and cost.

Charles Jencks is the Diaghilev of an experiment which involves many creative spirits. He is a tall, lean ascetic-looking American who trained as an architect and took to polemical writing and criticism. He is nothing if not an enthusiast and proselytizer for postmodernism. Today his interests revolve mostly around cosmic gardens and landscape design. It was back in 1988 that he and his late wife, Maggie Keswick, bought the house in Holland Park. There was a prelude at Cape Cod, Massachusetts, when in 1976–77 Jencks created the Garagia Rotunda, a hybrid of vernacular styles, classical allusions and witty juxtapositions. This Trianon of contemporary architecture was a design from scratch, whereas in London Jencks needed to adapt a

LEFT Vanbrugh meets Miami beach.

Victorian terraced house in a conservation area. Only at the back, the side of the house, and indoors could he allow his imagination a free reign.

The street was part of a planned set of Kensington crescents and squares for the Ladbroke Estate. The Hippodrome racecourse occupied the site until 1841, when its closure allowed James Ladbroke to commission Thomas Allom to plan a new residential area. William Reynolds was the architect who built the pleasant, spacious, brick and stucco semi-detached terraced houses that include the Jencks House. When Charles and Maggie Jencks began their adaptations to the house they saw it as a journey towards a symbolic architecture, not the culmination. Charles invented the iconographic programmes and Maggie kept it functional. The end result was a collaboration of many, notably Terry Farrell and Mike Fisher, with contributions from Eduardo Paolozzi, Michael Graves and Piers Gough.

The fun starts at the front door. It is a hominoid with head and hands, and the heart for a postbox. The head is Charles's own emblem, the 'Jencksiana', an arch window with a stagger motif, and it is used everywhere in the house both ornamentally and functionally. Enter the house and you are in a world in which everything has both a public and a private meaning. The entrance hall is the Cosmic Oval, a space panelled with mirrored doors that point north and south.

ABOVE LEFT The garden front.
ABOVE RIGHT The front door contains the first of many 'Jencksiana' windows.
RIGHT The Spring Room.

LEFT The Summer Room, with
Alan Jones's painting *Summer*.
RIGHT The Solar Staircase.

A mural by William Stok illustrates the evolution of the galaxies after the Big Bang and a dozen heroes of Jencks – including Hadrian, Erasmus and Thomas Jefferson. There are inevitably many references and layers of meanings. Jencks hero worships two of the great intellectual art historical iconographers, Erwin Panofsky and E.H. Gombrich. Visually we are in the world of Ledoux and Soane, with art deco/Biedermeier detail and fittings.

The visitor is invited to make a contribution to the house in the Cosmic Loo where a frieze of postcards can be rearranged or new ones inserted (the Postcard Game). At the heart of the house is the Winter Room, with a Michael Graves fireplace. After Winter comes the Spring Room. Spring leads us towards the outdoor world and the Sundial Room, with its giant window on to the garden that uses theatre machinery to take the glass up and down. A semicircular seating arrangement around the window is both intimate and Druidical.

The Summer Room is the dining room, all sunshine and light, where beige, maple and marble meet. Next to it is the Indian Summer Kitchen, where Jencks points out that the materials are not what they seem, '90 per cent fake, 10 per cent marble'. If modernism was about truth and beauty, postmodernism enjoys deception and the phoney wherever it can save money and allow symbolic resolution. The dining-room chairs (around the sun table) are made of medium-density fibreboard to look like maplewood. The kitchen takes Hindu architecture as its point of departure, with temples to fire and ice. The kitchen triglyph is made up of marbleized wooden spoons.

Perhaps the most dazzling part of all is the Solar Staircase. It is at the core of the house and structurally holds it together.

It is a tour de force. Mark Girouard, who wearied of the multiplicity of messages in the house, thought the iconography of the staircase, with the dual theme of the moon and the sun, the most effective because it is 'a simple but powerfully emotive one . . . and the symbolism is perfectly related to plan and decoration'.[1] Halfway up the stairs comes the Architectural Library, the only room in the house allowed to speak for itself. This playful room with toytown bookcases and pigeonholes for archives is the office and creative heart of the house.

[1] Mark Girouard essay in *Charles Jencks*, Toyko 1986, p. 111.

Girouard described the main bedroom as 'one of the most beautiful and original rooms of the century'.[2] Jencks calls it the Foursquare Room; his homage to Ledoux and Adam and the only room in the house that is quite symmetrical. The fantasy continues through the bathrooms and up to the top floor. Further elements deserve exploration. The jacuzzi designed by Piers Gough is based on inverting the dome of Borromini's S. Carlo alle Quattro Fontane: 'Heaven is sitting in a jacuzzi by Borromini eating foie gras' (Jencks). The Time Garden and Future Pavilion make a worthy background to the extraordinary side elevation of the house, where Vanbrugh meets Miami Beach.

[2] Ibid., p. 111.

If you still don't know what postmodernism is, this is it. Jencks has enriched the vocabulary of architecture and demonstrated that you can take the conventional London terraced house and make it a vehicle of personal expression and imaginative architectural ideas.

OPPOSITE The Architectural Library.
ABOVE The Foursquare Room.

MALPLAQUET HOUSE

136–139 MILE END ROAD

If irony can be affectionate, then Malplaquet House is irony incarnate. Its style lies anywhere between Cockney Cuzco and Mile End Road Baroque. The house of Tim Knox and Todd Longstaffe-Gowan in Stepney is a composite work of art in which their art collection, house and garden are entwined with their working lives. It is defined most strikingly by its profusion of pictures, sculptures and natural history; an antiquarian collection in the tradition of Hans Sloane, Sir Ashton Lever, Horace Walpole and Sir John Soane. It views the past through an eighteenth-century prism, using the artefacts of the nineteenth century but with a postmodern twist.

Tim and Todd have always loved ruins and the exotic. Both have Anglo-Irish roots and had peripatetic childhoods. Todd was brought up in the West Indies and South America, where he acquired a baroque sensibility and a

love of accretion. Tim was born in Africa and brought up in Nigeria and Fiji. They both came to England as children and responded to the forlorn state of country houses in the 1970s, the *sic transit gloria mundi* aspect of ruined pavilions and ivy growing through chapel windows. Tim was schooled near Petworth but had a teenage epiphany at the Norfolk houses of Gunton Park and Felbrigg. After a period at the RIBA Drawings Collection he joined the National Trust and today is Director of the Soane Museum. Todd trained as an architect but became a gardener and is the leading authority on London's historic gardens and squares. They met in 1988 and bought Malplaquet House together from the Spitalfields Trust in 1998. The house was in a state of extreme decay. Its resurrection has been a decade-long labour of love.

The house was built in 1742 by a speculative builder, Thomas Andrews, as one of three. Only two survive today.

RIGHT The upper landing bristles with moose and antelope heads in the manner of a country house trophy hall, while a plaster statue of St Rita of Cascia hints at another of the owners' obsessions.

OPPOSITE The dining room is lined with nineteenth-century portrait busts – a marmoreal company who compete for attention with painted portraits, including a large double portrait by Van Dyck.
LEFT The first-floor drawing room has comfortable kelim-covered sofas and portraits of recusant nuns.

The first tenant was a wealthy Jewish widow. The longest tenure was that of Harry Charrington, of the brewing family, 1794–1833. He made major alterations. After him the house was subdivided and shops were built over the front garden. It went into a long decline. Small businesses moved in, a bookmaker, a printer, and in 1910 the Union of Stepney Ratepayers, who were to remain in the house under various mutations until 1975. Despite their presence, the state of the house deteriorated rapidly, becoming unrecognizable under layers of additions and subdivision into small units. Wartime bombing raids further mutilated the building, which was repaired in 1951 using the £100 provided by the War Damage Commission. A young East End architect later to become famous, Richard Seifert, provided new shop fronts (it was then occupied by a typewriter rentals firm and a separate metal-foil printing business). By the late 1990s the building was so degraded that without the intervention of the Spitalfields Trust it would have been demolished.

The arrival of Tim and Todd was timely. Their aim was to restore the house but to preserve its atmosphere and the layered evidence of its history. Restoring the building was a priority but it also provided a foil for their already well-developed collections – which grew to fill the house. Weekly visits to Portobello Road Market, to flea markets and auctions, provided the accumulation of objects which give the house its Soanian appearance. The contents are in perpetual rearrangement and constantly being upgraded. They are apostles of art in the tradition of Ricketts and Shannon.

The hall, with its portrait of a vicar apostolic, antlers, death masks and stelae casts from Giza, leads to the Sarcophagus Room with its collections of portraits of nuns, something of a speciality of the house. The centrepiece is the giant chimneypiece made by Christopher Hobbs in 2002–3, with trophies of gardening, sheaves of architectural drawings, exotica from South America and Africa, an anthology of the owners' interests, including their dachshunds. 'Tiepolo, Prague and Palermo?' suggests Tim attempting to pin down the references.

The dining room, which was the typewriter shop, today holds architectural models in glass domes, Victorian busts and painted portraits against arsenic green walls. In addition there is a sedan chair bequeathed to Tim by Derek Sherborn, Van Dyck's unfinished double portrait of *Sir Arthur Hopton and his Brother Sir Thomas Hopton*, and the mitre of Henry, Cardinal Duke of York.

On the way upstairs is the cabinet, which contains natural history and curiosities from beyond Europe, a touch of Tradescant's Ark and the Pitt Rivers Museum. Skulls, devotional prints and stained glass complete the ensemble. The main first-floor room is the drawing room, with more recusant nuns, Victorian marble busts, eighteenth-century terracottas, mollusc-encrusted bracket-lights and a stuffed Kashmir goat. The fun continues in room after room, a crucifix bathroom, an obelisk study, the staircase with animal trophies *à la* Tatton Park. How many objects are there in the house? Nobody knows. Tim, who is Roman Catholic, enjoys the products of nineteenth-century devotion, oleographs,

plaster statues and *bondieuserie*, which are displayed with irony and affection in equal measure. The collection is a work in progress and no doubt there will be many more additions. The house is by any standards an inspiration and a reproach to those who live with fitted carpets and central heating.

OPPOSITE The remains of an interesting 1790s painted and papered decorative scheme still adhere to the walls of the study.
BELOW The bronze room contains – as well as bronzes – corals, portraits and an architectural model of an Italian villa.

SELECTED BIBLIOGRAPHY

NOTE

The literature on London houses was never as extensive as that on country houses. It opens with letter-writers and diarists like Samuel Pepys, John Evelyn and James Boswell, who frequently dined in them. Nobody retailed the gossip from London houses in the eighteenth century better than Horace Walpole. Surprisingly few foreign travellers left descriptions of them until the nineteenth century, when the German art tourists Johann David Passavant and Dr Gustav Waagen left impressively detailed descriptions of their contents.

A number of novelists used London houses as a setting: notably, Disraeli, Thackeray, Trollope, E.F. Benson, Henry James, Michael Arlen and Evelyn Waugh. Oscar Wilde set two of his plays in them and even Graham Greene, once he had adopted a child's eye view from the other side of the green baize door in *The Basement Room*, was not immune to their glamour. Equally interesting are the memoirs of those who visited or lived in them: Harriet Wilson, Lord Ronald Gower, Shane Leslie and Osbert Sitwell all come into this class.

We come to the rise of architectural history and the various descriptive histories of the subject. Pride of place goes to Beresford Chancellor's 1908 *The Private Palaces of London*. The magazine *Country Life* photographed a great number of them from the 1930s onwards and their archives, later used by John Cornforth in his *London Interiors* (2000), remains one of the best sources of photographs and articles. In 1945 John Summerson produced his brilliant *Georgian London*, which although not specifically about houses remains the best short account of their development within its confines; I refer to it frequently in the text. Christopher Simon Sykes produced his pioneering *Private Palaces* in 1985 and David Pearce his *The Great Houses of London* the following year. The *sic transit gloria* aspect of the subject was emphasized by Oliver Bradbury in *The Lost Mansions of Mayfair* (2008); and we await Joseph Friedman's *The Treasure Houses of London*, in preparation. Apart from all these excellent studies, what made writing this book easier is the existence of *The Survey of London*, with its deep and considered scholarship. These volumes cover about two-thirds of the houses in this book and it would be impossible to praise the recent volumes too highly. Finally, a word of admiration and gratitude for the six volumes of 'Pevsner' that cover London, as revised by Bridget Cherry and Simon Bradley.

GENERAL

Bird, Sir James (editor), *Survey of London*: vol. 8, *Shoreditch*, London 1922

Bradbury, Oliver, *The Lost Mansions of Mayfair*, London 2008

Chancellor, Beresford, *The Private Palaces of London*, London 1908

Colvin, Howard, *Biographic Dictionary of British Architects: 1600–1840* (4th edition), New Haven and London 2008

Cornforth, John, *London Interiors: From the Archives of Country Life*, London 2000

Cox, Montague, and G. Topham Forrest (editors), *Survey of London*: vol. 14, *St Margaret, Westminster, Part III, Whitehall II*, London 1931

Crewe, Quentin, *Crewe House*, London 1995

Godfrey, Walter (editor), *Survey of London*: vol. 4, *Chelsea, Part II*, London 1909

Greenacombe, John (editor), *Survey of London*: vol. 40, *Knightsbridge*, London 2000

Harris, Eileen, *The Genius of Robert Adam: His Interiors*, New Haven and London 2001

Mordaunt Crook, Joseph, *The Rise of the Nouveaux Riches: Style and Status in Victorian and Edwardian Architecture*, London 1999

Pearce, David, *The Great Houses of London*, London 2001

Pevsner, Nikolaus (with Simon Bradley), *London 1: The City of London*, London 1997
  (with Bridget Cherry), *London 2: South*, London 1983
  (with Bridget Cherry), *London 3: North-West*, London 1991
  (with Bridget Cherry), *London 4: North*, London 1998
  (with Bridget Cherry and Charles O'Brien), *London 5: East*, London 2004
  (with Simon Bradley and John Schofield), *London 6: Westminster*, London 2003

Roberts, Sir Howard, and Walter Godfrey (editors), *Survey of London*: vol. 23, *Lambeth: South Bank and Vauxhall*, London 1951

Saunders, Ann, *The Art and Architecture of London* (2nd edition), London 1988

Sheppard, F.H.W. (General Editor), *Survey of London*: vol. 27, *Spitalfields and Mile End New Town*, London 1957
  Survey of London: vols 29/30, *St James's Westminster: South of Piccadilly*, London, 1960
  Survey of London: vols 31/32, *St James's Westminster: North of Piccadilly*, London 1963
  Survey of London: vols 33/34, *Soho*, London 1966
  Survey of London: vol. 37, *Northern Kensington*, London 1973
  Survey of London: vol. 39, *The Grosvenor Estate in Mayfair*, Part I (General History), London 1977
  Survey of London, vol. 40, *The Grosvenor Estate in Mayfair*, Part II (The Buildings), London 1980

Summerson, John, *Georgian London*, London 1945

Sykes, Christopher, *Private Palaces of London*, London 1985

Thorold, Peter, *The London Rich*, London 1999

Weinreb, Ben, and Christopher Hibbert, *The London Encyclopedia*, London 1983

Waagen, Gustav, *Treasures of Art in Great Britain* (3 vols), London 1854

Wedd, Kit, *Artists' Houses in London: Holbein to Hirst*, London 2001

SPECIFIC HOUSES

Lambeth Palace
Dodwell, C.R., *Lambeth Palace*, London 1958
Haslam, Richard, 'Lambeth Palace, London I & II', *Country Life*,
    18 and 25 October 1990
Lambeth Palace Official Souvenir Guide, London (n.d.)

Ashburnham House
Field, John, *The King's Nurseries: The Story of Westminster School*,
    London 2007

10 Downing Street
Jones, Christopher, *10 Downing Street*, London 1985
Seldon, Anthony, *10 Downing Street*, London 1999

Wimborne House
Binney, Marcus, *The Ritz Hotel*, London 2006
Sitwell, Osbert, *Laughter in the Next Room*, London 1949
Watkin, David, Nicholas Thompson and others, *A House in Town*,
    London 1984

44 Berkeley Square
Mowl, Timothy, *William Kent*, London 2006

The Mansion House
Jeffery, Sally, *The Mansion House*, London 1993
Worsley, Giles, 'The Mansion House', *Country Life*, 11 November 1993

Coventry House
Lejenne, Anthony, *The Gentlemen's Clubs of London*, London 1979
Seward, Desmond, 'The St James's Club' in Philip Zeigler and
    Desmond Seward, *Brooks's, A Social History*, London 1991

3 Grafton Street
Binney, Marcus, 'Taylor's Grafton Street, I & II', *Country Life*,
    12 and 19 November 1981
Garnier, Richard, 'Grafton Street, Mayfair', *The Georgian Group
    Journal*, vol. XIII, 2003, pp. 201–272
Gilman, Michael, a seven-page manuscript history of 3 Grafton
    Street produced in 1996 for the present owners

Spencer House
Friedman, Joseph, *Spencer House*, London 1993
Martin Robinson, John, and Jane Rick, *Spencer House* (guidebook,
    new edition), London 2006

Home House
Carter, Miranda, *Anthony Blunt*, London 2001
Cooper, Douglas, *The Courtauld Collection*, London 1953

Stratford House
Lightbown, Ronald, *An Architect Earl: Edward Augustus Stratford*,
    London 2008
Riches, Hugh, *A History of the Oriental Club*, London 1988

Dover House
Cecil, David, *The Young Melbourne*, London 1939 (new edition 1954)
Stroud, Dorothy, *Henry Holland: His Life and Architecture*,
    London 1966
Turner, Jane (editor), *The Dictionary of Art*: vol. 10 (entry on Lord
    Dover), London 1996

Sir John Soane's Museum
Knox, Tim, *Sir John Soane's Museum, London*, London 2009
Stourton, James, *Great Smaller Museums of Europe*, London 2003
Summerson, John, *Sir John Soane's Museum* (revised edition),
    London 1966

Apsley House
Bryant, Julius, *Apsley House: The Wellington Collection*, London 2005
Longford, Elizabeth, *Wellington: Pillar of State*, London 1972

Regent's Park Villas
Mordaunt Crook, Joseph, 'The Villas of Regent's Park',
    Country Life, 4 and 11 July 1968
Tuttle, Maria, and Marcus Binney, *Winfield House*, London 2008

Lancaster House
Gower, Lord Ronald, *My Reminiscences*, London 1883
Yorke, James, *Lancaster House*, London 2001

Kensington Palace Gardens
Girouard, Mark, 'Town Houses for the Wealthy: Kensington Palace
    Gardens I & II', *Country Life*, 11 and 18 November 1971
Stansky, Peter, *Sassoon*, New Haven 2003

Dudley House
Nevill, Lady Dorothy, *Reminiscences*, London 1906
Stevenson, Michael, *Art and Aspirations, The Randlords*,
    South Africa 2002
Waagen, Gustav, *Treasures of Art in Great Britain*, vol. II,
    London 1854
Walford, Edward, 'Apsley House and Park Lane', in *Old and New
    London*, vol. IV, London 1878

The Speaker's House
Cooke, Sir Robert, *The Palace of Westminster*, London 1987
Stones, Elizabeth, and others, *The Speaker* (house guide,
    first published London 1982), current edition 2009
Riding, Christine, and others, 'The Speaker's House', in David
    Cannadine and others, *The Houses of Parliament*, London 2000

4 Cheyne Walk
Connolly, Cyril, *The Condemned Playground*, London 1945

Linley Sambourne House
Nicholson, Shirley, *A Victorian Household* (based on the diaries of
    Marion Sambourne), London 1988
Robbins, Daniel, *Linley Sambourne House* (guidebook), 2003

Tower House
Dakers, Caroline, *The Holland Park Circle: Artists and Victorian
    Society*, New Haven 1999
Handley-Read, Charles, 'Aladdin's Palace in Kensington: William
    Burges's Tower House', *Country Life*, 17 March 1966
Mordaunt Crook, Joseph, *William Burges and the High Victorian
    Dream*, London 1981
Mordaunt Crook, Joseph (editor), *The Strange Genius of William
    Burges 'Art Architect', 1827–1881*, for the National Museum of
    Wales, Cardiff 1981

Astor House

Betjeman, John, and others, *2 Temple Place, Headquarters of the Smith and Nephew Group*, London (n.d.)

Hall, Michael, 'A Palace for a Plutocrat: 2 Temple Place', *Country Life*, 4 January 2012

Incorporated Accountants' Hall, its History and Architecture, London 1953

Quiney, Anthony, *John Loughborough Pearson*, New Haven 1979

Brazilian Embassy

Life of Robert George Earl of Plymouth (1885–1923), privately printed, Cambridge 1932

Rubens, Antonia Barbosa, *The Brazilian Embassy in London*, London 1995

Saint, Andrew, unpublished short history of 54 Mount Street held at Brazilian Embassy

Debenham House

Calloway, Stephen, and Lynn Federle Orr (editors), *The Cult of Beauty: The Aesthetic Movement 1860–1900* (catalogue of exhibition at the Victoria & Albert Museum), London 2011

Garland, Madge, 'No. 8 Addison Road, Kensington', *Country Life*, 20 November 1975, pp. 1388–1391

Musson, Jeremy, 'Debenham House', *Country Life*, 17 February 2005

6–9 Carlton House Terrace

Bloch, Michael, *Ribbentrop*, London 1992

Vickers, Hugo, *Gladys, Duchess of Marlborough*, London 1979

Davie, Michael (editor), *The Diaries of Evelyn Waugh*, London 1976

Nicolson, Harold, *Sir Arthur Nicolson, Bart., 1st Lord Carnock*, London 1930

Notes and Records of the Royal Society (6–9 Carlton House Terrace): 22, 1967, 20–36; 23, 1968, 1–3

64 Old Church Street

Powers, Alan, *Serge Chermayeff: Designer, Architect, Teacher*, London 2001

Zevi, Bruno, *Erich Mendelsohn*, Bologna 1982, English translation 1985

Television talk between John Gloag and Serge Chermayeff, Avery Archive

2 Willow Road

Powers, Alan, *2 Willow Road* (National Trust guidebook), London 1996

10 Milner Street

Piper, Myfanwy, *Reynolds Stone: Engravings*, London 1977

Spitalfields Houses

Severs, Dennis, *18 Folgate Street: The Tale of a House in Spitalfields*, London 2002 (revised 2008)

Richard Rogers House

Cook, Peter and Richard Rogers, *Richard Rogers + Architects*, London 1985

The Jencks House

Adamson, Glenn and Jane Pavitt (editors), *Postmodernism: Style and Subversion* (catalogue of exhibition at the Victoria & Albert Museum), London 2011

Girouard, Mark, essay in *Charles Jencks*, Toyko 1986

Jencks, Charles, *The Language of Post-Modern Architecture*, New York 1977
Towards a Symbolic Architecture, The Thematic House, London 1985

INDEX

Page numbers in *italic* refer to captions to illustrations.
Page numbers followed by the letter n refer to footnotes.

ACKNOWLEDGEMENTS

I am grateful to the following for assistance, permissions or reading of texts regarding individual houses:

The Archbishop of Canterbury and Andrew Nunn (Lambeth Palace)
Dr Stephen Spurr (Ashburnham House)
Simon Gimson and Terence Dormer (Marlborough House)
Sir Gus O'Donnell and David Heaton (10 Downing Street)
Stephen Boxall and Ian Leggatt (Wimborne House)
Joanna Ismail (44 Berkeley Square)
Peter Bignell (The House of St Barnabas)
The Lord Mayor, Alderman Michael Bear and Wayne Garrigan
     (The Mansion House)
Karveen Puddoo and Chris Hughes (Coventry House)
Peter Bustin (3 Grafton Street)
Lord Rothschild and Jane Rick (Spencer House)
Mike Lynch (20 St James's Square)
Andrew Richardson (Home House)
David Swain (Stratford House)
Gervase Hood (Dover House)
Tim Knox (Sir John Soane's Museum)
Lord Douro and Josephine Oxley (Apsley House)
Charles Kendall (Regent's Park Villas: The Grove)
Sarah Morris and James Yorke (Lancaster House)
Vice Admiral Charles Style CBE, Col. Andrew Gordon-Lennox,
     Andy Lennard (Seaford House)
Peter Williams (Kensington Palace Gardens)
Lakshmi and Usha Mittal (18–19 Kensington Palace Gardens)
Kees van der Sande (Dudley House)
The Hon. Mr Speaker, Peter Barratt, Malcolm Hay (The Speaker's
     House)
Victoria Press (4 Cheyne Walk)
Daniel Robbins (Leighton House and Linley Sambourne House)
HE The Italian Ambassador and Nicola Todaro Marescotti (The
     Italian Embassy)
Jimmy Page and Paul Reeves (Tower House)
Richard Hoare and Mary Rose Gunn (Astor House)
HE The Brazilian Ambassador and Helena Maria Gasparian (The
     Brazilian Embassy)
Nasser Abdallah and Susanna Chancellor (Debenham House)
Paul Killik and Katalin Sinkovics (46 Grosvenor Street)
Keith Moore (6–9 Carlton House Terrace)
Lady Hamlyn and Barry Gillion (64 Old Church Street)
Joseph Watson (2 Willow Road)
Courtenay Inchbald (10 Milner Street)
Simon Wedgwood (Spitalfields Houses)
Lord and Lady Rogers (Richard Rogers House)
Charles Jencks (The Jencks House)
Todd Longstaffe-Gowan and Tim Knox (Malplaquet House)

The following gave me excellent advice of a general or
particular nature:

Colin Amery
Rose Balston for admirable research
Charity Charity
Sue Gladstone (picture research)
Dr Michael Hall
Jonathan Hewlett (Savills)
Dr Susan Jenkins
Simon Jervis
Jonathan Marsden
Sir Michael Pakenham
Professor Alan Powers
Nicholas Thompson
Michael Turner

I am grateful to three friends who kindly read the introduction
and made sound suggestions:

Joseph Friedman
John Goodall
Jeremy Musson

The following kindly read the entire manuscript and suggested
many improvements:

Mark Girouard
Dr John Martin Robinson
Dr Rory O'Donnell
Sarah Rutter
Professor David Watkin (my Cambridge tutor, still reading my
     essays more than thirty years later)
Dr William Zachs

Finally, I am very grateful to my agent, Georgina Capel (Capel
& Land), who introduced us to Frances Lincoln. It has been
nothing but a pleasure working with the editor Jo Christian, whose
enthusiasm has been stimulating and sustained. My assistant Devon
Cox at Sotheby's typed the manuscript and Becky Clarke has done a
marvellous design job.

Without question my greatest debt is to the photographer, Fritz von
der Schulenburg, for his brilliant photographs. He was a delightful,
efficient and easy collaborator. We were both hugely assisted by
Karen Howes of Interior Archive, who arranged all the shoots and
saw us through the numerous bureaucratic hurdles to be overcome.

PICTURE CREDITS

The publishers have made every effort to contact holders of copyright works. Anyone we have been unable to reach is invited to contact the publishers so that a full acknowledgment may be given in subsequent editions. For permission to reproduce the images on the following pages, and for supplying photographs and artworks, the publishers thank those listed below.